The Awakened Aura

"Kala is an amazing metaphysical teacher, with a deep understanding of her subject. In this well-written, personal, and heartfelt book, she reveals the secrets of the auric field, its power and meaning. This is a very useful and easy-to-understand guide."
—Amy Zerner and Monte Farber,
authors of *The Soulmate Path*
and *Chakra Meditation Kit*

"Kala Ambrose has written the definitive work on the human aura and its many aspects. This is not just a book about how to see and feel auras; it is a book about what the aura is, and how it affects the way we move through life on all levels. A must-read."
—Sandy Anastasi, author of *The Anastasi System of Psychic Development*

"Ambrose provides us with a fantastic 'field guide' to auras, writing with clarity, authority, and insight as she presents us with everything we need to know about what it truly means to be creatures of energy and light. This is important information for a transformative time as we head into an age of expanding awareness and consciousness. I highly recommend this wonderful book."
—Marie D. Jones, author *of Destiny Vs. Choice: The Scientific and Spiritual Evidence Behind Fate and Free Will*

"Through the wise words and simple techniques of this beginner-friendly guide to the aura, Kala Ambrose not only manages to enlighten her readers on a very human level, she actually does so by inspiring them to rise above it. Thus, teaching us all the most basic of Universal principles: in order to connect with the spirit of others, we must first awaken our own."

—Marguerite Manning, author of
*Cosmic Karma: Understanding Your
Contract with the Universe*

"Kala draws on her personal experiences and her extraordinary sense of perception to clearly present the evolution of auras since she first began seeing them as a child. Using her gift, she clues us into what we might expect in the future. *The Awakened Aura* provides helpful ways to tune into, reenergize, and revitalize our own subtle bodies at a time when we need it most."

—Debra Moffitt, author of *Awake in the World:
108 Ways to Live a Divinely Inspired Life*

"Kala Ambrose writes as she speaks—from her heart. Her words resonate with a profound truth that will awaken your soul to the spellbinding treasure trove of wisdom that is you."

—Elizabeth Harper, author of
Wishing: How to Fulfill Your Heart's Desires

"A brilliant, well-written book by Kala Ambrose. I highly recommend it and expect it to be a classic on all healers' shelves."

—Colette Baron-Reid, author of *The Map:
Finding the Magic and Meaning
in the Story of Your Life*

The Awakened Aura

About the Author

Kala Ambrose (Raleigh, NC) is an intuitive empath, inspirational speaker, and voice of the highly acclaimed *Explore Your Spirit with Kala Show*. An award-winning author, Kala writes for the *Huffington Post* and is the national metaphysical spirituality writer for Examiner.com. Visit her online at ExploreYourSpirit.com.

To Write to the Author

If you wish to contact the author or would like more information about this book, please write to the author in care of Llewellyn Worldwide, and we will forward your request. Both the author and publisher appreciate hearing from you and learning of your enjoyment of this book and how it has helped you. Llewellyn Worldwide cannot guarantee that every letter written to the author can be answered, but all will be forwarded. Please write to:

Kala Ambrose
℅ Llewellyn Worldwide
2143 Wooddale Drive
Woodbury, MN 55125-2989

Please enclose a self-addressed stamped envelope for reply,
or $1.00 to cover costs. If outside the USA, enclose
an international postal reply coupon.

Many of Llewellyn's authors have websites with additional information and resources. For more information, please visit our website at http://www.llewellyn.com.

EXPERIENCING THE EVOLUTION
OF YOUR ENERGY BODY

The Awakened Aura

Kala Ambrose

Llewellyn Publications
Woodbury, Minnesota

FIRST EDITION
First Printing, 2011

Book design by Bob Gaul
Cover art: Woman © iStockphoto.com/Shannon Keegan,
    Lotus © iStockphoto/s.m.Art designs
Cover design by Lisa Novak
Editing by Nicole Edman
Interior illustrations © Mary Ann Zapalac

Llewellyn Publications is a registered trademark of Llewellyn Worldwide Ltd.

Library of Congress Cataloging-in-Publication Data
Ambrose, Kala, 1966–
   The awakened aura : experiencing the evolution of your energy body / Kala Ambrose. — 1st ed.
      p. cm.
   Includes bibliographical references (p.   ) and index.
   ISBN 978-0-7387-2759-2
   1. Aura I. Title.
   BF1389.A8A43 2011
   133.8'92—dc23
                    2011021153

Llewellyn Publications
A Division of Llewellyn Worldwide Ltd.
2143 Wooddale Drive
Woodbury, MN 55125-2989
www.llewellyn.com

Printed in the United States of America

Also by Kala Ambrose

9 Life Altering Lessons
Ghosthunting North Carolina

To Tim:
Your love lets my spirit soar, and the late night talks guide me gently back to Earth. Thank you for taking this adventurous journey with me and for being my rock through it all. My world shines brighter every moment I spend with you!

To Brandon:
You've been a wonderful teacher and gift wrapped up in one phenomenal package; truly you are a blessing in my world.

To my Friends and
Fans of the *Explore Your Spirit with Kala Show,*
and to the Students of
the Wisdom Teachings:
We are all One and I honor each and every one of you along the path. This book is dedicated to each of you, the beautiful souls that you are. Together on this journey, we will continue to glow and grow!

Contents

List of Exercises

List of Illustrations

Introduction

My Color-Filled
Life Path as a Psychic
and Aura Reader

We are all One, One Energy, from One Light.
Let us band together as humans with love for all
of humanity, living each day in harmony as we
explore our spirit.

—Kala Ambrose

Have you ever had a feeling about someone that you couldn't explain, but the feeling was so strong that it affected how you felt about that person? When we're at a loss to explain how we feel, we might describe this person as "dark" and "foreboding" or the opposite, such as having a "sunny disposition" or being "a ray of sunshine" in our lives. Perhaps you hadn't realized it, but these feelings are proof of your metaphysical abilities!

For thousands of years, artists in ancient Egypt and later in Rome and other parts of Europe attempted to paint the energy they sensed around a person, such as a halo around an enlightened being or dark shadowing around someone who is consumed with sadness or guilt. While artists strive to depict these energies and others search for words to describe them, I've been lucky enough to see this phenomenon with my own eyes my entire life. Since my earliest memories of childhood, I have seen colors and rays of light around people—what are known as auras.

I arrived in this lifetime with memories of past lives as a wisdom teacher, sharing what is known as the esoteric mystery teachings. I lived and shared these teachings in ancient Egypt, Greece, India, and Ireland, and I continue to teach them again in this lifetime. As a wisdom teacher, showing others how to see the aura in its many expressions is one of the most valuable things I can do. Seeing auras can lead to self-actualization in the body, mind, and spirit fields. When we have conscious awareness of who we are as spirit beings, doors open to new levels of existence on the earthly plane and in the higher realms. Not only are we able to understand ourselves on a deeper level and further develop into supernatural beings of light, we are also able to understand our fellow humans on a profound, connective soul level.

I've spent my current lifetime dedicated to pulling all the knowledge and wisdom from my previous lifetimes into my conscious fields so that I could access these teachings freely and share them with others. This lifetime has given me psychic abilities, including seeing the aura, being intuitive, seeing ghosts and beings from other planes, being able to astral travel, having prophetic and teaching dreams, connecting and working with spirit guides and the elders, possessing empathic and psychometric abilities, and (most importantly) having a heart chakra field that is wide open to compassion and love for humanity.

Over the years, I've studied metaphysical sciences such as astrology, tarot, traditional Feng Shui, magic, and the wisdom of master teachers of the ancient esoteric systems. Along with my esoteric inner work, I've dedicated my life to teaching these skills to others with my school of the mysteries, the Temple of Stella Maris, and lecturing and holding workshops around the United States. In my esoteric outer work, I write books and a national column and host the *Explore Your Spirit with Kala Show*, where I've conducted hundreds of interviews with world-renowned authors, artists, teachers, and researchers in the metaphysical, spiritual, paranormal, and scientific realms. I've discussed our ancient past, worked to reveal lost history, and shared what is to come for our future. Most importantly, I've worked to maintain and hold the vision that Spirit is everywhere. I believe that through sharing and teaching the gifts that each of us has received in this lifetime and others, great healing and awareness will come to this planet, which will lead to the evolution of humanity as superpowered beings.

I believe that one of the most important factors in this evolution is the ability to see and sense the auric fields. When you can see the aura and the energy bodies surrounding the aura, you can see how people are truly feeling, regardless of what they are saying vocally. You can see their state of mind, their state of health, and their state of being. The various fields also show the karmic ties they bring with them, the guides who are surrounding them, and the destined path on which they are heading. The aura fields are like open books describing who we are on all levels. As open books, we do not have to shield who we are, for it is on display for all the world to see, providing a great freedom to be ourselves and live in the moment with the conscious awareness that "who we are" is a constant process of change and evolution. The end result is more incredible and exciting than many of us have ever imagined.

Can You Feel the Love?

Many people say to me that they are not able to see auras and wonder if they truly exist. Seeing the first layer of the aura is relatively easy to accomplish. In the workshops I teach, 90 percent of the people I work with are typically able to see the first layer of the aura by the first or second exercise. While it is fairly easy to see the outline of an aura (the etheric body is first viewed as a white border around the body), understanding what the colors inside the auric fields represent can be more challenging.

Are you wondering if you are sensitive to energy fields? Consider these situations in which you were aware of energy that you could not see with your physical eyes:

- Have you ever walked into a room and felt the mood of the room coming from the people inside, without knowing what the current conversation is about?

- Have you ever walked into a building and felt uncomfortable for no apparent reason, but you wanted to get out as soon as possible?

- Have you ever met someone for the first time and immediately felt uncomfortable and preferred not to be around them? Or have you warmed up to someone immediately and found yourself wanting to spend as much time as possible in their company?

- Have you ever played the game where you are blindfolded and rely on sensing energy to see where someone else is located in the room and how close you can get to them?

- Have you ever taken a tai chi or other type of martial arts class? One of the first exercises you learn is to sense your personal chi/energy field. Students are taught how to feel the energy radiating off the body and how to harness the energy between their hands, forming it into a ball. They are also taught deep-breathing exercises in order to raise the energy field and expand it. These lessons connect directly into the auric field and are a great way to connect with your personal energy.

• Have you ever been deep in thought and not paying attention to your surroundings and suddenly you "felt" someone looking at you? The person staring at you was directing their energy at you and your energy field, and the auric body reacts to the energy ripple, sending a message to your conscious mind to pay attention. It is being protective in this response, so that the mind can take the next step to discern whether the person is friend or foe and react accordingly.

In these situations and many others, you have felt the energetic auric field around a person. There are hundreds of examples regarding the auric fields and their energy, and one of the most compelling stories comes from the sleeping psychic, Edgar Cayce.

During the last year of his life, Edgar Cayce began work with his friend Thomas Sugrue to write a book about his work with auras. This book was intended to be a full discourse on auras and colors, including Cayce's notes on how he learned the meanings of specific colors and shapes in the aura via observation of his clients. Unfortunately, his health took a turn for the worse and he died in early 1945. Due to Cayce's untimely demise, the compilation of his work and study of the auras was simply made into a twenty-page pamphlet entitled *Auras: An Essay on the Meaning of Colors*. To this day, *Auras* is a popular reference guide containing helpful information, including how the colors in the aura are connected with the planets and musical notes.

As a psychic who saw auras, Cayce shared his most traumatic experience in regards to seeing auric fields. One day Cayce was on a high floor of a high-rise office building and pushed the button for the elevator in order to return to the first floor. When the elevator opened in front of him, he was completely caught off-guard—he could not see the aura of any person on the elevator. This surprised him, as he was used to seeing an auric field around people wherever he went. Puzzled by what he saw, he continued to stare in surprise and did not enter into the elevator car. The elevator doors closed and the cable of the elevator snapped, plunging all of the people in the car to their deaths.

The auric field was absent around the people on the elevator because it was preparing the physical body for death. Rather than its normal state of extending outward, the aura begins to pull inward into the body to gather the essence and soul of the person as death nears. This act assists the consciousness in the shift from the physical plane of existence of the body into the higher realms of the spirit.

Seeing Auras: A Psychic's Viewpoint

From my own experiences in reading auras, I've found that the auric body typically maintains a basic form that resembles an egglike oval shape around the body. Emanating from this body is a beautiful white light along with a wide variety of colors, shapes, and (at times) swirls and patterns. While it is fairly easy to learn to see an aura, knowing what the colors and images surrounding the aura represent requires intuition, practice, and an understanding of the spiritual planes and fields around the body.

Each individual creates a distinctive pattern in their auric field comprised of their thoughts, emotions, energetic manifestations, and thought forms. The aura has an electromagnetic frequency that is sensed by others and radiates at a unique level. When people resonate at a similar auric frequency level, they naturally feel more comfortable around each other and find it easier to connect on the physical, emotional, and mental levels. On the flip side, people whose auric vibrations differ greatly in frequency tend to experience more conflict with each other and find it more difficult to communicate. In some ways, because they are coming from such different energetic standpoints, it's almost as if they are speaking two different languages. In short, birds of a feather flock together and, while opposites attract, the opposing energy fields can create conflicts and difficulties.

Human beings are essentially made of light and energy. As we come into contact with another person, our auras engage and intermingle with each other. This can lead to many positive experiences, which stimulate and enhance the aura. It can also lead to negative experiences, which can draw too much energy away from the auric field and leave a person feeling depleted. With a greater understanding of how the aura functions, it's easier to recharge the aura to keep it running at an optimum level.

There are seven main layers to the aura, which are also sometimes referred to as *bodies* or *fields*. There are many people who can see these auric fields. Some intuitives see them with their physical eyes. Others see the fields through their third eye, and some only sense the auric fields. A small number of people are able to see all seven auric fields, while the majority of people can see one or two fields only. Some psychics are more attuned to see "dis-ease" before it enters the physical body, while others see the energy in motion around the person, which reflects their general well-being.

A person may also see emotional distress in the auric field, or catch glimpses of the akashic records being worked through in this lifetime. *Akashic records* is an ancient Sanskrit term that refers to a database of records, a library of sorts, that records all actions in the Universe. While each person is here on the earthly plane in a physical body, part of their essence and soul remains in the higher planes. A metaphysical energetic cord connects the higher planes to the earthly plane and attaches to the soul of each person as it resides inside the physical body. These cords move energy back and forth between the planes. Also contained in these fields of energy are the records of each thought, word, action, and deed that we generate while in a physical body. These records are transported back to the akashic library, where they are stored; when we pass on from the earthly plane and return to the spiritual realms, we visit the hall of akashic records to review our lifetime. From this study, we can see whether we generated more positive karma and what we created from our actions.

In my work as a wisdom teacher, I teach students how to see and read auras. We discuss the types of auras, their condition, and how to heal an aura that has become damaged due to shock, stress, or other harmful situations. In this line of work, I continue to experience new revelations when giving aura readings for people.

What has been most astounding and exciting in my work is that, in the past ten years, I've seen new structures forming around the auras, which I have never seen before in the auric fields.

My theory on this new design in the auric field is that we are in a quickening period. We are evolving on an energetic level and our auric bodies are being re-created right before our very eyes. What I see is that the energy bodies around us are being reconstructed and are opening up to allow more light and energy than ever before to flow through our bodies. In addition, the grid around the auric body is expanding and the structures are becoming more crystalline in appearance. From my research, only one other time in history references the energy around the human body changing; this was in the time of ancient Egypt, when the high priestesses prepared to communicate with their gods and goddesses. As we draw nearer to the astrological Age of Aquarius—which is symbolized by the water bearer in the heavens pouring the wisdom of the gods back down to Earth—I am struck by the correlation in what I see manifesting in our auric bodies. I believe the energy fields around our bodies are being prepared to receive higher and stronger vibrations of energy. The effects will allow for more energy to come into our physical bodies, allowing us to live longer and with greater vitality. It will also allow for greater mental capacity and increased psychic ability.

In the past four years (2007 through 2011), I have seen these alterations gain even greater momentum. The structures surrounding the auric field and energy bodies are different in people according to their age and physical, emotional, mental, and spiritual state of well-being. What I have seen forming in all stages of life is overwhelmingly positive and awe-inspiring—so much so that I felt compelled to write this book to share with others what I am seeing in the auric fields and explain how these changes are leading to the evolution of our light bodies!

Auras, like so many natural gifts given to us, are powerful conductors of energy. Used consciously with an understanding of their capability to be a pure vessel to store and transmute energy, we can use auras to transform ourselves in body, mind, and spirit. In many ways, these changes represent the symbolic sarcophagus used in ancient Egypt, allowing us the opportunity and sacred space in which to regenerate, transmute, and transform our physical, emotional, mental, and spiritual bodies. From what I've observed and discerned, and according to the pace of the structures forming in the auric bodies, many people have the potential to become superpowered human beings by the year 2020. I'll go into this exciting auric evolution in chapter 11.

Seeing the Light through the Eyes of a Child

But let's back up a step, to my beginning in seeing auras. These events began in my childhood. I was born with intuitive and empathic abilities. As a child with empathic ability, I didn't quite understand what was happening to me. I would experience the intensity of emotions around me until I got a severe stomach ache, caused by taking in everyone's emotions through my solar plexus chakra. I would end up ill for several days during family holidays, when I would absorb all the energy in the home from people's emotions, which run high during family events! Later, as I came to understand what I was feeling, I learned how to block some of the intense energy in the room so that I would not absorb as much of it. While I have become skilled in this work, I still find it difficult to be in crowded places for an extended period of time.

Along with sensing the energy fields around people, I also saw their colorful auras. As a child, it never occurred to me that others did *not* see auras around people, animals, and trees. For comparison, when you step outside into the sunshine and the light is so bright that it makes you squint, do you run over to other people and ask, "Do you see the light outside? Is it so bright that it makes you close your eyes a little? Is the light yellow in color to you?" No. You don't ask these questions; you just assume that what you experience is what others are also experiencing, especially when you are young.

My first inkling that I was seeing something different from everyone else occurred when I attended a Catholic elementary school. We had been assigned to color a picture of our home and family. While coloring each family member, I colored outside the lines, portraying the colors of the aura around each person. My teacher, who was a nun, criticized my picture and chastised me for not doing a good job since I had colored outside of the lines and thus was not following instructions.

As an empath, I sensed that my teacher was very displeased with my work, but I could not understand why. I didn't understand that my teacher could not see auras, and so I assumed that she was criticizing my artwork and skill in drawing and coloring. On that day, I decided to never draw or paint again, as I evidently must be horrible at doing both. This was especially sad given the fact that my mother was an artist who drew and painted beautifully, but I went home too embarrassed to tell her what had happened. In my mind, she would be horrified that her own daughter had drawn a picture so badly that it was an embarrassment to the nuns.

Growing up Catholic often brings along a lot of guilt and an emphasis on shame. At that time, I felt that I had brought shame to my mother with my poor artwork. I had no idea that the nun was only critiquing me on the fact that the color was "supposed" to stay inside the lines that had been drawn. For quite some time, my young empathic heart was bruised.

As an empath, it's important to have time away from others to restore energy. Thus, my favorite activity in childhood was to read, especially about anything to do with magic, the paranormal, and ancient history. Each week I would go to the library with my grandmother and check out as many books as they would allow. I read every book I could find about the history of ancient cultures and mythologies from around the world. I would occasionally be found carefully crossing out sentences and editing what I felt was incorrect in these books. I remember feeling quite upset at how the stories were being misconstrued.

At a young age, my intuition rebelled strongly against what I was reading about the history of women. I was a precocious child at best. My mother said that I carried a deep and wise look in my eyes and exuded the energy of a soul wanting to get things done. There was always the sense that I was patiently waiting for my small body to grow so that I could begin what I was here to do. In addition to skewed history books, reading children's stories only perplexed me further. I would ask my mother and father, "Why, in all the fairy tale books, do the mothers always die and the stepmothers are always cruel, and why are witches always bad?" Snow White, Cinderella, Sleeping Beauty, and even Bambi—in every story, the mother dies. I also could not understand why all the girls only wanted to be a princess and never a queen, who ruled through her own power.

Seeing auras and sensing energy fields also led me into a great conflict with what I was being taught in Catholic school. I was being told that to connect with God, one had to go to church. Yet, I could see the aura and energy of the trees, flowers, and animals, and around every person I saw, no matter where I was. The entire world was bursting with life. Every part of the world was colorful and alive and full of energy. At night, as I said my prayers and lay down to sleep, beings of light would visit with me and I would see people from the Other Side. While I didn't fully understand what was occurring at the time, I was on my journey to become a teacher of the ancient wisdom teachings and to share these ancient lessons, as I have done many lifetimes before.

Today, I see how strong the energy of the Wise Woman and the Divine Feminine ran in me, and I've connected with my past lives and understand their role in who I am today.

This color-filled journey brought me to my life path vision:

> *Spirit does not exist in just one location; rather it*
> *is all encompassing, living within and amongst*
> *us in each moment, thought, and action. I believe*
> *that Spirit is raised to its highest level when*
> *individuals gather with wisdom, compassion, and*
> *a discerning desire to provide service to humanity.*

Each Person Has a Unique Auric Field

During my experiences of reading auras, I've found that they are almost as unique as fingerprints. While some characteristics are similar in form, including some shades of color, each individual creates a distinctive pattern in their auric field. This field is created mostly by four energetic vibrations: the individual's thoughts, their emotions, manifestations of spiritual energy flowing into the body, and the creation of thought forms that have been around the person for a significant amount of time. The overall result is incredibly beautiful. I am continually astounded by the beauty and energy of the patterns I see in people and what they are able to create in their aura as a result of their thoughts and emotions.

When viewing the aura, I have little doubt that each person is truly unique, with a distinct purpose to be here, and that everything we do on a daily basis matters and has a purpose. The auric body works as a container to hold and distribute our energy inside of the body and to project it outward to the higher energy fields and planes.

As human beings, we are creators with a vast abundance of energy within our reach. With each individual thought, word, action, and deed, we release an energetic pulse that forms its own distinct imprint. These energetic creations are stored in the auric body, while also flowing outward to be felt by others.

Basically, each thought and action we take creates a ripple of energy that flows from the auric body and interacts with others in our field. This creates a unique pattern of cause and effect, of which no two are the same. If you have ever wondered if what you do and who you are makes a difference in this world, *rest assured that you do make a difference, and in most cases you are unaware of how much of an effect you have on others on a daily basis.* This can be broken down to the simplest of acts: a soft touch, a smile, or lasting eye contact. The aura contains all of this information and stores it for you so that you can create what you think about and send it outward onto the physical plane (and then on to the higher planes of existence). Each action, thought, emotion, and deed that you create and then experience on this physical plane is recorded and stored in your energy body. When you pass over from this lifetime, you will have the opportunity to review all of this information and observe how your actions affected others.

Each person arrives on the earthly plane with a divine plan to accomplish while here in each lifetime. If you wonder what you are meant to do in this life, the easiest way to connect with your destiny is to think back to when you were a child and could do and dream about anything you wanted. What did you love to do and what did you do solely because you enjoyed it so much? When you remember what those things were, you are well on your way to connecting with what you are here to do in this lifetime.

Getting Started

Throughout this book, we'll explore what the aura, chakras, and energy bodies do on a daily basis. We look at how the aura is formed in each infant during pregnancy and how it continues to develop and grow throughout each lifetime. We'll explore how to see auras, expand our energy fields, heal our energy bodies, and connect with the energy as it moves from the higher planes down into our energy bodies and anchors in the chakras. Perhaps most importantly, we'll take a look at how our auras are evolving, creating new crystalline structures that are preparing our bodies of light to evolve into new superpowered human beings, which will affect the physical body as well.

In this new century, we are moving into an age of enlightenment. The energy of the Divine Feminine is being released in all her glory and I believe we will once again see a renaissance period, where great art, architecture, philosophy, literature, and science will develop and flourish. During this decade, the greatest minds will stir to share, illuminate, build, and create works and ideas that will be marveled at around the world. Part of why the evolution of humanity is going to grow so exponentially is because the evolution and revolution are ongoing from the higher planes into our auric bodies. The future is here; prepare to be changed on multiple levels and discover new talents and gifts that are yours to receive. This is a very exciting time, and my hope is that learning to see and understand auras will allow you to see and understand the changes that are already on their way for us.

I believe that the only way to understand life is to experience it fully. We are on this earthly plane to experience, learn, grow, and evolve. I continue to do my best to fully explore everything life has to offer and while my spirit soars on the other planes, I also believe it's important to have a firm grounding on the earthly plane and to live, laugh, and love here to the fullest extent.

From my journey in this lifetime, I have come to the realization that we are the sum of our experiences, both from this life and from our past lives. I look forward to sharing the color-filled path with you in this book.

One

THE LIFE FORCE
KNOWN AS THE AURA

Know thyself, and know thy body, thy mind, thy soul are as the three dimensions in which ye find thyself.

—Edgar Cayce

Scientific research has expanded exponentially in recent centuries, but the wisdom teachings of mystics have been around for thousands of years. Finally, these two seeming opponents have joined forces to study and further illuminate information and data on the energy fields around the body. Science is now admitting that there is more to a human being than just the physical body. The exploration of gene therapy and cellular research, such as is written about in Bruce Lipton's book, *The Biology of Belief,* has revealed that each cell is filled with energy drawn from a larger field around the body.

Every living being—including plants, animals, and humans—has been given a life-force containment field called an *aura.* The aura is an energy field with seven layers and is comprised of white light and all colors of the spectrum. This field forms an oval shape around the body and emits light and color, which can be seen by some people naturally. In many cases, people can see the white light auric field around a body after only a few hours of instruction and practice.

The auric field is, in actuality, the radiance of the soul. The human aura is the radiation or emanation of energy as contained in each body. This emanation can grow in strength and size and expand the fields and layers around the auric fields according to individual development. The human aura is both physical and spiritual in nature and is affected by emotional, mental, physical, and spiritual energy.

The human aura indicates the vitality and health of the body, mind, and spirit because it envelops all of the bodies. It is affected by physical illness, stress, emotional trauma, and negative thoughts as well as love, joy, spiritual growth, meditation, and positive thoughts and affirmations that it receives over the lifetime. Too much stress can cause the aura to wear thin and crack; too much negativity and anger can cause the aura to become thick, hard, and heavy, forming a wall around the field; too much sadness and grief can cause the aura to become too porous, to the point where it leaks like a sponge. In its healthiest state, the aura is malleable—it easily expands and contracts according to circumstances and allows energy and light to move freely into and out of the auric fields. When in a healthy condition, the aura can be trained to expand to great distances. It has been reported that certain spiritual masters can expand their aura for miles around them. The aura continuously changes colors according to the state of the emotional field. It also reflects the colors radiating the energetic vibration of a person, as well as their true nature.

Your aura responds to your every emotion and thought. Sympathy, empathy, love, desire, jealousy, anger, joy, and depression are sensed and expressed through the auric fields. How we feel about ourselves is expressed through our emotions, our thoughts, and our actions. We believe that we keep this inside and that no one is aware of how we feel, but the aura reflects this energy, which some people can see with the naked eye and others only feel energetically. You can feel the influence of a person through their aura. The auric field creates a vibe, an energy field, which radiates and expands outward and affects each person you come into contact with. If your aura is radiating strong energy, people will be drawn to you, because your auric field is expressing a vibe of personal magnetism. If you are feeling depressed, the aura pulls inward, grows thin, and has to spend its time pulling in energy to sustain the fields, which leaves little room for it to expand and develop. When a person is angry for a long period of time, the energy hardens in the aura and can become almost impenetrable, which slows the flow of light and energy through the fields. Instead, energy builds inside like a volcano and erupts when enough pressure allows it to explode through the hardened auric wall.

When we learn proper breathing techniques in combination with meditation and spiritual practices, we can gain more control over our aura and learn to expand it, raise its energy, and increase the amount of magnetism, energy, and light in its fields.

As Within, So Without: Chakras and the Auric Fields

The first three auric fields are closest to the body and are the easiest for people with intuitive abilities to see. While the aura can be viewed outside of the body, it also connects into the physical body at energy centers called chakras. *Chakra* is an ancient Sanskrit word that means "wheel." This describes the whirling motion that each of the chakras makes inside the body. Chakras are also referred to as gates and portals. The ancient Sanskrit teachings are the first recorded references to the chakra system and energy fields and how they operate. Detailed information on the chakras appears in the *Upanishads*, which is from around the seventh century BCE. In the Western world, we begin to see

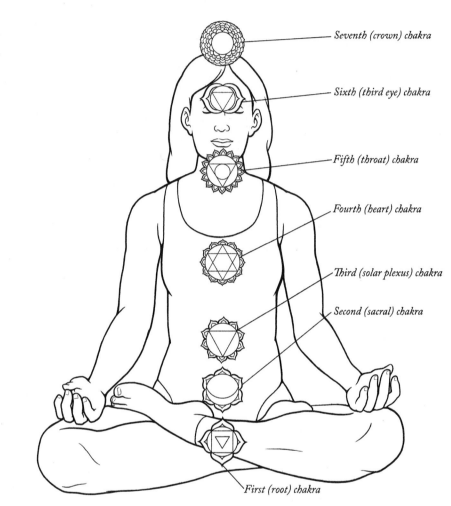

Seventh (crown) chakra

Sixth (third eye) chakra

Fifth (throat) chakra

Fourth (heart) chakra

Third (solar plexus) chakra

Second (sacral) chakra

First (root) chakra

The seven chakras.

references to the aura and energy fields with Pythagoras around 500 BCE, as he observed the aura and discussed how it was connected to healing the body from physical disease. During this time, healing temples were established to treat illness at the body, mind, and spirit levels.

As the seven chakras begin their work in the body, they spin endlessly as they receive energy brought in from the energy fields of the aura and then circulate the energy throughout the body. When functioning at their highest potential, each chakra is able to move energy freely and in balance at a healthy rate. When they become overloaded, the chakra's ability to rotate diminishes; the chakra is holding too much of the incoming energy and is overwhelmed as it continues to receive energy, but cannot move the energy outward through the nervous system, organs, and other chakras at the same speed. The energy cannot be processed throughout the body to maintain good energy flow and physical vitality, and problems can occur with physical health and emotional distress.

The chakras become sluggish when the nervous system becomes overloaded with stress, exhaustion, overwork, and mental and emotional trauma. When this occurs, some people seek to have their chakras balanced and realigned in order to clear some of the negative energy and jump-start the rotation of the chakras again. While this is certainly helpful, it is only the first step; if the person does not remove the stress that is causing the chakras to overload, the situation will only repeat itself over and over again.

The nervous system runs throughout the body and connects to the chakras, forming meridians that are subtle energy channels in the body. The nerves—referred to in Sanskrit teachings as *nadis*—collect the energy from the chakras and distribute the flow of energy throughout the body through channels, called the Ida and Pingala. The nadis connect not only with the seven major chakras, but also with the minor chakra points throughout the body, of which there are thought to be more than 350. Eastern medicine acknowledges and works with these pressure points using acupuncture and acupressure to stimulate and heal the body.

The Auric Delivery System

The auric field is comprised of seven major layers, which are also described as energy fields. There are layers beyond the seven, but in our current phase of evolution as humans, it is extremely rare to see

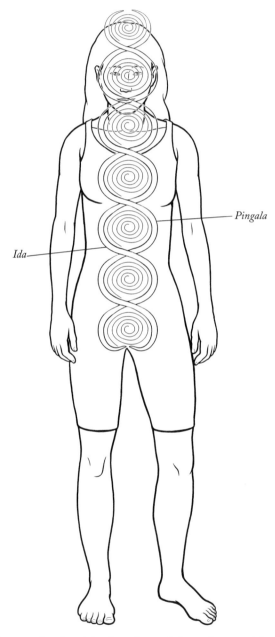

Energy nadi paths swirling from the root chakra to the crown chakra.

or interact directly beyond the first seven layers in our physical state. When we pass on and travel back to the Other Side, all of these layers travel back with us and the higher layers are more engaged with our soul when we reside on the higher planes.

While we think of our emotions and thoughts as emerging from within us (coming from the heart and the brain), the truth is that we receive these thoughts and feelings first outside of us in our energy bodies, and they are then drawn down into our physical body. The layers of the aura deliver the information from our higher self and the spiritual planes and filter it down through the auric layers. The final destination is the physical body, where information is delivered through the chakras and nervous system.

And this process occurs with every thought we have. The next time you find yourself deep in thought, notice your body posture. Many people tilt their heads up slightly toward the sky or look upward with their eyes. Others bring their hands together with the tips of the fingers touching each other to form a pyramid shape, which helps focus and draw the energy inward. When we focus our energy to generate a brilliant idea, it is described as our "eureka" or "aha" moment. The inspirational thought we receive is coming to us from the higher realms, delivered through the mental layer of the aura. The ancient Greeks described this as the Muses whispering in their ears. In cartoons, this event is frequently depicted as a shining light bulb appearing over the head of a person who is receiving a "bright idea."

Many ancient cultures wore hats shaped like an upside-down cone, which worked to harness energy from the spiritual ethers and draw it down into the cone to be received by the recipient. The witch's hat is an example of this pointed cone hat style. The pyramid shape has tremendous potential to attract, focus, and harness energy and pull it down into the desired area. The cone-shaped "dunce cap" that students who were doing poorly in school once had to wear represents another symbol of this geometric shape, intended to deliver focus and clarity to the brain.

Another example of how the auric fields first receive information and then filter it down to the physical body is when people describe feeling a "state of shock" or express that surprising news came as a "blow" to them. The information is first received and distributed through the layers of the aura. The emotional layer of the aura captures some of the intense energy in this field to lessen the pain felt in the physical body due to the incoming emotional response. The aura is only a filter and thus can only slow down how quickly the energy travels, so the person still experiences the physical shock and pain, which often manifests as an upset stomach, headache, and other overwhelming effects on the nervous system.

When in proper working order, the aura does a good job of filtering energy so that our nervous system, glands, organs, and chakras can handle stress and other stimulating mental and emotional information. However, problems arise when our aura becomes overly stressed and is not able to function properly, or when we receive so much shock and stress in a short period of time that the fields are simply not able to cope with the overwhelming flow of energy.

The Forming of Auric Patterns

I have never seen the exact same aura pattern on two different people, and I see something new each time I view a person's aura. The best description that I've been able to provide for the aura is "the emotions in motion," due to the fact that the colors in the aura constantly change according to the thoughts and feelings a person is experiencing.

Consistent patterns found in the aura are created by long-held thoughts and beliefs, both positive and negative. The good news is that if you change your thinking at the core level, you can change these patterns. The bad news is that if you are not aware of how to do this, you keep creating an energy field that you may not care for and will continue to wonder why your life is spiraling in a negative direction. In the coming chapters, you'll learn not only how to see the aura, but also to understand what you are seeing and determine what you can do to make significant and powerful changes within your energy field.

What I See in Our Light Bodies

Beginning around the age of four, whenever I would look at a person, I would see light emanating from within and around their body. Most people had an average amount of light coming from them, not extremely bright but not dim either, and this light remained fairly consistent when I would see them each time. The light around each person would change the most when they experienced a volatile emotional reaction. The subtle colors in the layers of the aura would also change frequently according to their emotions and thought patterns from moment to moment.

As a child, I was sometimes fascinated by what I saw around the adults and at other times was very frightened. I also discovered that I didn't even need to see the person to sense their energy. Before they would enter a room, I would sense their energy field and have a general idea of how they were feeling, what kind of mood they were in and—being intuitive—what was on their mind.

Beginning in my childhood, I began to make mental notes of what I saw and felt in the auras of people. One of the first things I remember noticing was that the auras of other kids produced more light, on average, than the adults. The only major changes I would notice in most kids' auras occurred when they were angry, upset, or very tired. The rare times I saw something very different in a child's aura, I later came to understand that the person had a mental disability or was a victim of some kind of abuse.

I had no idea that what I was looking at was called an aura; I simply saw it as the colorful lights around people. Being raised Catholic, I had seen artwork and statues displaying glowing halos on spiritual people, so I wasn't really surprised to see this with my own eyes. However, during my elementary school years, I began to realize that the adults could not see the colors and patterns around other people or that they were ignoring them. The adults were usually unaware of what others were thinking and feeling and they often lied to other adults who had no way to discern whether or not they were telling the truth. I once tried to tell a teacher about another teacher who was lying and she punished me when I tried to explain how I knew the person was being dishonest. After that, I kept my revelations to myself.

Over the years of observing and learning, I was able to discern distinctive patterns in the aura on the various levels and understand what they meant. There are multiple layers to the auric field and they reflect how we are feeling on the physical, mental, emotional, and spiritual levels. Understanding what these layers do and how they operate can change the way you think about who you are as a person, as you begin to see yourself as a being of light. Fine-tuning these layers can enhance your life experience and expand your connection to all living things on the earthly plane and beyond.

Two

WHAT'S BEEN WORKING
ON OUR AURAS

Mind is the Master-power that molds and makes,
And Man is Mind, and evermore he takes
The Tool of Thought, and shaping what he wills,
Brings forth a thousand joys, a thousand ills: —
He thinks in secret and it comes to pass:
Environment is but his looking-glass.

—James Allen

Reading the aura of your body and the bodies of others can be helpful in many ways. The aura can indicate the health of the body as well as the condition of the mind and soul. In its most healthy state, the aura should surround the body with a distinctive shape while allowing a level of flexibility. This can be compared to a filter: When a filter is clean, it maintains its natural shape and is porous, allowing air or water to move freely in and out as it functions and does its job. When too much debris becomes attached to the filter, it clogs.

The result is that water or air is not able to pass through easily. In the same sense, auras can become clogged with negative energy.

The auric body operates much like the physical body in that they both require maintenance and care to run at their maximum efficiency. They will both do their best to operate at full capacity regardless of how much we help them. Just like water, nutrition, rest, and exercise are required for the physical body, the aura also relies on nutrients to replenish its energy. Two of these sources are mandatory for the aura and built in to our system, so that our "etheric battery" can recharge and replenish the aura. Just like the human body requires water and food, there are functions the aura must have to exist. Can you guess what these mandatory functions are that charge your aura?

They are breathing, which is the active process of moving energy in and out of the body, and sleeping. When we sleep, the restoration process known as our etheric battery charges. Once this energy containment field in the aura is fully recharged, it then begins to heal the multiple layers around the body, working its way through to the physical body to assist with repairs and restoration. One of the best things you can do for your body and your auric fields is to get a good amount of quality sleep each day.

The Natural Rhythm of the Aura

The Western world has interfered with the natural rhythms of the mind, body, and spirit by imposing a new calendar and clock onto modern society. The aura and etheric body suffer according to this new time schedule. In the past, people woke naturally with the movement of the sun and most cultures enjoyed a brief nap in the afternoon. Nap time allowed the physical body to shut down for an hour or so, so that the mental and emotional bodies could absorb and digest the information gathered from the first part of the day and process it while the etheric battery recharged the layers. The result was that people felt energetic and were more relaxed and tolerant, because they were following the natural process and healing techniques provided by the energy bodies.

The longer a person goes without sleep, the more distressed the physical body and the surrounding energy bodies become, because they are unable to recharge back to full capacity. The aura can restore some energy through meditation by consciously pulling energy in from the higher planes into the body. This is beneficial, but to fully restore, the body and the aura must have sleep to recharge. In our fast-paced, hectic world, sleep is often not enough to fully repair the bodies, due to mental and emotional stress, poor diet, and illness, all of which put a strain on the body and energy fields. It is important to learn not just how to recharge the aura and the energy bodies, but also how to enhance the field of the aura to a greater degree.

Cause and Effect: Why Big Changes Are Occurring in the Aura

With proper rest, fresh air, and nutrition, the aura will usually restore itself each evening. There are circumstances, however, that deplete the reserves in the aura and put it under great stress. Trauma or shocking events including war, abuse, and other long-term stressful situations place a great strain on the aura. Everyday living conditions can also put a strain on the auric fields.

Beginning in the twentieth century, the toll on our aura bodies began to increase. The Industrial Revolution was in full swing and factories and manufacturing were revolutionizing the Western world. People began to move en masse to cities and worked long hours in poorly ventilated conditions, including factories and skyscrapers with enclosed circulated air systems. Before the Industrial Revolution, people worked long hours as well, but they spent some of this time in nature and did a variety of activities with breaks in between. They also ate hearty, organic food harvested right from their local land.

As this situation changed and more people began moving into the cities, food had to be processed and brought in from other areas in order to feed the crowds of city people. To keep up with the new supply and demand, slaughterhouses were created in large numbers. As a result, the quality and freshness of food declined. It also became necessary to create preservatives to allow food to stay fresher for longer periods so it could travel on trucks and trains and survive the stocking time required in the newly created grocery stores.

During this period in the twentieth century, the United States went through the Great Depression, a decade-long period of poverty and stress, which affected each person living through these conditions. Many Americans had lived through World War I already, and as they recovered from the Great Depression, World War II soon had them sending their sons off to war. During this time, women went to work in the factories in larger numbers to pick up the slack from so many men being called away to war.

After World War II, the Baby Boom era began, which also expanded the economy. The new focus was innovation, and the boost to the economy was to create new inventions and appliances that could be sold to the consumer. The vision was to create an easier life for people; women would have to spend less time cooking and cleaning since machines did the work, and people could escape the cramped quarters of city life and live farther away from the city in newly created suburbs. They would travel on new highways to work at jobs in other cities in their new cars. Some would be given sales routes consisting of several states where they would travel by planes, trains, and automobiles to reach new customers with new products.

A major expansion occurred at this time—phones in every home, cars in every driveway, televisions in every living room, and a large array of appliances in the home, including refrigerators, washing machines, and small appliances. On a larger scale, airports were expanding in addition to freeways and interstates, and people and commerce were on the move. This opened up a new variety of interstate commerce, which moved produce and goods from one side of the country to another and expanded global imports, as goods could now be flown in fresh rather than travel for long periods on ships.

Two of the biggest innovations in the kitchen during this time were created in order to save time previously used for cooking, and these two innovations have made a significant impact on the auric bodies and fields: frozen dinners and the microwave. Included with these innovations were factory-packed and -sealed canned foods. This progressed over time into a wide variety of frozen foods, and the era of the microwave as a daily cooking tool—to heat and cook meals in minutes rather than hours—was not far behind.

As the new trend emerged, local merchants such as bakers and butchers were replaced with corporate grocery stores. In the 1980s, the advent of enormous discount chain stores established a new way to gather, process, and consume food.

You may be asking yourself at this point, "I thought I was reading a book about auras. Why am I reading about economics and history?"

I am sharing a brief history of economics and technological innovation because it has had a direct and profound effect upon our aura and chakras. **Unless we understand how outside stimuli affect our energy fields, we can't fully comprehend how to heal and repair the aura.**

The past century has affected our auric bodies on a greater scale than ever before experienced in humanity. As we spend more time indoors in offices and workspaces under fluorescent lighting and in recirculated air, we do not have the same access to breathing fresh air and absorbing sunlight as we did before. In addition, the nutritional energy provided in fresh foods, which were previously picked fresh and consumed right from the farm, has also been removed. Beyond the lack of nutrients from foods that have been sprayed with pesticides and then stored, freeze-dried, preserved, and overcooked, we are also now radiating our foods with microwaves. It appears that this is set to become a greater problem in the twenty-first century while overfarming and poor sanitary conditions are causing e. coli and salmonella outbreaks, and genetically altered foods and seeds are manipulating and changing the genetic compounds and structures of the foods we consume.

We are denying our energy bodies what they need most to operate at full capacity: exposure to sunlight, exposure to fresh air, healthy nutritious foods fresh from the earth, and time to rest. In addition, due to our increasingly stress-filled lives, many people are not sleeping well at night or for as many hours as they need. This leaves the auric fields with little to work with in order to enhance the bodies and generate energy. The fact that they manage to do so at all is an amazing testament to the design and capability of the auric bodies.

While sharing the history here of how industrialization has changed how the Western world eats, breathes, and sleeps, I must also state that I enjoy many of the luxuries our culture has created. I'm all for innovation and progress, but there is the old Latin phrase: *caveat emptor*, or "buyer beware." Technological innovations and progress move at a fast pace and not all of the potential outcomes and pitfalls are considered during the drive to create. The responsibility then falls to each of us to connect with our intuitive side and determine which lifestyle choices are best for our health and well-being.

Along with the change in nutrition and access to nature, the stress of living and working in the city takes a toll on each person. For some, the work in a factory setting was a daily grind full of repetitive motions for hours under dangerous conditions and with little time for extended breaks.

Others entered the corporate world, where the pressure was on to perform and work long hours in order to advance. Both types of work pulled people away from nature and away from seeing a job to completion. When working on the farm, one would sow the seed, water the seedling, and tend to the plant until the harvest, when the product would be taken to a local market. There was a beginning and an ending, and while farming is very stressful and hinges upon weather conditions and pests, there is a sense of value, connection, and completion to it, along with down time during the winter to rest and recuperate from the hard work of the year. In contrast, workers on assembly lines—and indeed in many modern workplaces—work repetitively on one aspect of a part of the whole and don't receive the emotionally and psychologically rewarding experience of seeing a completed product. The effect of repetitive work can be exhausting and demotivating.

In the corporate world, people can become paper pushers and are distanced from the people they are working to serve. One example could be a conglomerate insurance company that deals in large numbers of claims. Rather than having workers interact directly with the individual policy owners, new policy guidelines are implemented to deal with each situation as a case number, far removed from the actual experience and pain and suffering of the person seeking service from the insurance company. This might be the only way that many of these workers can come to peace with the decisions they are forced to make in order to meet the bottom line of the company directive. The insurance company's balance sheets may benefit from this separation, but it is not healthy for the customers and workers to be cut off from each other.

When people are pulled away from interacting directly within their community, they lose their sense of belonging and connection. A feeling of detachment and isolation occurs, beginning at the soul level and spreading through the auric fields. Once the soul becomes despondent from the lack of connection and harmony between what the person does for a living and what their core moral and spiritual beliefs are, it takes a toll on the person and their mental and emotional well-being. As most people know, there is little worse than dreading going to work each day. And studies are showing that job satisfaction in the United States is at an all-time low, just as unemployment numbers are on the rise. Many people who are displeased with their current occupations feel they aren't able to find another position, and so they feel "stuck" in an unhappy situation. It's the sad truth that an unfulfilling job is often better than no job at all.

In order to continue with an unsatisfying job, a person must grapple with and pull away from their conflicting feelings. This is what some would call their "conscience" speaking to them. It is saying, "This is not how I should live or what I should do." In order to keep functioning in a position where we do not feel energized by our work, we have to shut down our feelings and change our thoughts to convince ourselves that what we are doing is okay or that it doesn't really matter what we are doing so long as we earn a paycheck. This creates a new and potentially dangerous pattern in the body, mind, and spirit, because **what we think, we believe and what we believe, we become.**

When people experience conflict with what they are doing each day in order to make a living, they are forced to disconnect with part of themselves in order to do the job without feeling overwhelming guilt or shame. The daily internal struggle is enormous and has a dramatic effect on the physical, mental, emotional, and spiritual bodies, and the auric fields are directly affected by these thoughts and emotions.

When we pull away from the restorative energy of time spent in nature and ignore our inner natural instincts, it becomes easier to make decisions that our higher selves do not agree with. A dangerous cycle is created—the further we pull away, the more detached we become. This became a clear and present danger in the twentieth century and appears to be a growing trend now in the twenty-first-century lifestyle.

Three

Revealing the Seven Layers of the Aura

Here at the fountain's sliding foot,
Or at some fruit-tree's mossy root,
Casting the body's vest aside,
My soul into the boughs does glide:
There, like a bird, it sits and sings,
Then whets and combs its silver wings;
And, till prepared for longer flights,
Waves in its plumes the various light.

—Andrew Marvell

The aura can be seen and sensed on multiple levels. In some layers, psychic "dis-ease" can be viewed before it fully enters the physical body and becomes disease. Symptoms of emotional distress and conflict are present in the auric field, as well as glimpses of the akashic records and karmic debt being worked through in this lifetime. Let's explore further to see how each layer moves energy and supports our body, mind, and spirit.

The Seven Layers of the Aura

Layer One: The Etheric Body

This layer operates as the life-force battery of the body. It is the closest to the physical body and is typically the first auric field that people are able to see. It extends about two inches from the physical body and connects inwardly to the first (root) chakra, as well as to the organs of the body. The etheric layer is also what one sees when viewing the aura of plants and trees; it is the life-force energy surrounding each living object. The etheric body stays with the physical body until it dies. It is attached to the organs, glands, nervous system, and the chakra system.

When viewed, the etheric body most often looks bluish-white in color. This aura can appear very clear when the person is in optimal health. Typically, this auric field appears light and shiny. When it becomes cloudy, dullish, or gray, it indicates that the person may be in poor health, depressed, or is abusing drugs or alcohol, both of which dull and desensitize the auric fields.

Modern advances in the medical field have developed ways to keep our physical bodies alive and functioning in severe circumstances using life-support machines to keep the lungs breathing and other bodily functions working. However, if the etheric body stops operating, there is no machine that can keep the body alive. When the etheric body pulls away from the physical body, the life force is extinguished, and there is no longer any energy being delivered to the body. Just as this body attaches to the nervous and chakra systems and to the internal organs, it also has cords that stretch outward from the auric fields into the highest spiritual planes, where part of each soul remains. When the life force is extinguished, these cords detach from the physical body and pull the auric layers back up into the soul in the higher planes.

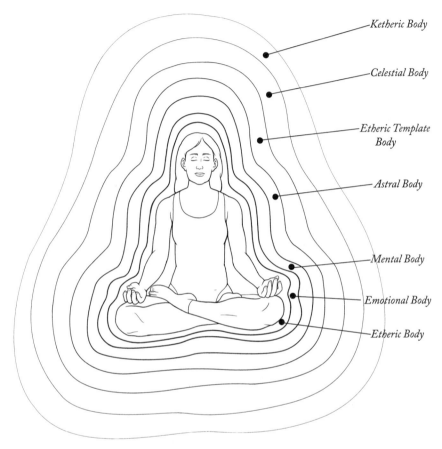

Ketheric Body

Celestial Body

Etheric Template Body

Astral Body

Mental Body

Emotional Body

Etheric Body

The seven layers of the aura. (Not to scale.)

They bring with them all the physical, emotional, mental, and spiritual imprints from the life of that soul on Earth and deliver this information to the akashic records in the higher realms.

Layer Two: The Emotional Body

Expanding about four inches outward from the first layer, the emotional auric body connects inwardly to the second (sacral) chakra. This layer of the aura changes the most often in color, as it is affected directly by our emotional state. I often refer to the aura as "emotions in motion." When most people see colors in the aura, the emotional field is what they are viewing. This field is especially easy to view when the person is in a highly emotional state.

Once you can easily see the white light of the etheric auric field around the body, it becomes easier to see the colorful emotional second layer. In general, the brighter and clearer the colors are in this layer, the more balanced and healthy the person is emotionally. Muddy colors typically indicate emotional stress and trauma. The emotional layer should appear clear and bright, which means that it is in good working order and emotions are being filtered in and out of the layer into the other bodies at a good pace.

When this layer appears thick and dense, it indicates prolonged periods of emotional distress. This person and their auric field has become overloaded and overwhelmed, and action must be taken to clear the fields so that the person does not suffer to the point of physical stress and disease. If this blockage is not treated, this field has the potential to become thick and hard, so that it is difficult for energy to move in and out, or soft and spongy, where the layer leaks energy and light.

When any one of the auric fields is not working properly, it affects the other fields and the physical body, as each field relies on the others to gather and distribute energy. For this reason, it is never a good idea to shut down emotionally or mentally; when this field is shut down, it slows the energy distribution to all of the auric bodies and makes each field work harder to get around the problem. It may seem like a good idea to a person under emotional stress to try to protect themselves by shutting down their feelings, for example. In actuality, they are punishing themselves and extending the pain. They have slowed the energy flow, which in turn slows positive energy from reaching them as well. In addition, shutting down bottles up the pain and suffering rather than allowing it to work its way through the bodies in order to be released.

Layer Three: The Mental Body

The size of the mental body field varies greatly. Personally, I've seen them range from as little as two inches from the emotional layer to as expansive as twelve inches. The average size appears to range between four and eight inches. The mental body connects to the third (solar plexus) chakra and is also referred to as the "seat of will."

Mystics have long stated that there is a brain of sorts located in the solar plexus, and science is now beginning to agree with this school of thought. Ongoing experiments have discovered there is a cluster of brain nerves in the stomach area, which range to more than a hundred billion nerve cells. Researchers now believe that this "second brain" saves information about physical reactions to mental processes and sends out signals when making decisions later, including affecting the emotions of happiness and sadness. Professor Wolfgang Prinz of the Max Planck Institute for Psychological Research in Munich has joked that this discovery could lend new credence to the phrase "gut reaction."

This gives rise to further scientific consideration on the studies of foods considered to be "brain food," like omega-3 fatty acid. There are foods that can enhance the chakras, as discussed in chapter 4, as well as foods that stimulate the brain. Further study needs to be considered as to which foods may best enhance the "brain" found in the stomach/ solar plexus area.

The mental layer of the aura is where our thoughts and ideas originate. The thoughts are then filtered from our higher mind through the mental layer and delivered into the solar plexus and third chakra level to be processed. At this level, the information travels upward to the brain in the skull to process and communicate the thought outwardly through speech or action.

Layer Four: The Astral Body

The astral layer is primarily a connective bridge that carries energy from the higher planes of existence and delivers it into the lower three layers of the mental, emotional, and physical. However, this is the secondary function of this body; its primary function is to connect with the fourth (heart) chakra and deliver the pure energetic and vibrational energy of love from the spiritual planes into the heart chakra. By design, the astral body extends about twelve inches from the physical body and, when fully engaged, can expand much farther.

In babies and young children, this connection is wide open. This is one of the reasons why children are so easily capable of unconditional love. The soft spot on the skull is connected to the cords and energy fields. In this state, with part of the skull open, they are receiving a great flow of energy and information from the various planes. Because of this open connection, many children are very intuitive up until the age of 7, when the soft spot of the skull fully closes. Kids younger than 7 also frequently report seeing imaginary friends and describe deceased family members who visit them.

Young children are innocents who are fully connected with their higher selves with little barrier between the fields. Between the ages of 4 and 7, as they are exposed to the world via school and other encounters, they experience stressful and judgmental situations, and they begin to close down this connection as a protective measure. For some it begins earlier when they are placed in preschool.

By the time a person reaches the age of 21, the physical, emotional, and mental layers are fully formed. It then requires a conscious decision to open these layers back up to full capacity in order to cross the astral bridge and connect again on a deeper level with the fourth layer and open the heart chakra. This act often happens spontaneously when a person falls in love. When this occurs, the energy soars and reaches across the astral bridge to interact with the heart chakra, and a series of chemical, alchemical, and electrical reactions take place. Unless the heart chakra and fourth layer is connected fully, which comes from raising the energy of the person into a state of unconditional love as opposed to emotional love, the energy will ebb and flow, as it is not fully established in the fourth layer. This is why love can run hot and cold; when it exists mainly in this level in the physical, mental, and emotional bodies, it is affected by the whims and desires of these bodies. When love is fully anchored in the heart chakra, it is not attached to judgment, desire, or emotional impacts and thus radiates with a spiritual quality.

But you can't just skip to the good stuff (true spiritual love) without doing the work on lower levels. A system of checks and balances is put into place, and one must begin at the first auric layer and work upward, cleansing and purifying the three lower layers first, so that they are clear to receive and deliver the energy efficiently. It is indeed a grand design. Think of a time when you first fell in love and how you felt. You had increased energy, everything in the world felt wonderful, and your emotional and mental state was positive. This is what it feels like when you have cleared and expanded the first three layers of the body, and you have the capability to feel like this at any time.

It is quite a treat to view this layer of the aura when a person is in love, as the effect is similar to watching an elaborate fireworks display.

Layer Five: The Etheric Template Body

The etheric template body contains a full imprint of the physical body. At present, only a small number of people are able to view this layer of the aura. It is, however, extremely valuable to be able to view the etheric template body, as it indicates physical disease and illness in the physical body. A person who can read the etheric template can work as a medical intuitive and provide information on where disease is manifesting in the body, which is beneficial to both the person and the doctors who are treating them. If caught in time by a medical intuitive, the disease can be seen before it enters the physical body. At this stage, action can be taken to head off the illness. As more people become able to view the etheric body, the possibilities are astounding as to how helpful and revolutionary this could be for human well-being. The medical community would have the potential to expand holistic health practices, and healing care and clinics could be established where people could have medical intuition readings before illnesses become physical problems.

The etheric template contains the pattern that was dictated for how our physical body was intended to be formed in this lifetime, including our genetic code, hair color, skin color and texture, eye color, height, and so on. It is a much larger field than the etheric layer of the body, averaging about two feet in size. The etheric template is a carbon copy of the physical body. It indicates the current state and health of the body while also retaining the image of how the body should look when it is in perfect health. Many people have reported seeing a loved one appear to them after death, seeming to be in perfect health and young—around their early 30s. This is because once a person dies and leaves their physical body, they project their true physical and etheric template. People have reported seeing their loved ones in this healthy state, including ones who had lost limbs but appear with their limbs restored and fully functional. The etheric template always holds the image and energy of our true physical form.

We can use the power of focused thought and energetic manifestation to connect with this layer and bring this energy down into the body, in order to restore it physically. The etheric template is connected to the fifth (throat) chakra and with our power of speech. We are the only beings on Earth who were given this unique power of speech. This gives us the ability to manifest. It has been written that "in the beginning, there was the Word" (John 1:1). With words, we manifest and create. What we speak, we become. Each person has the power on an individual level to change their energy and their world by carefully and deliberately choosing their words.

Layer Six: The Celestial Body

The celestial body expands, on average, three to four feet from the other layers. This body is very light and ethereal and its duties are focused on the spiritual realms. It is connected to the sixth (third eye) chakra. This is the realm where we are able to connect intimately with the Other Side for communication. When the third eye is open, we "see" through this realm, which is much more expansive than what we view through our physical eyes. The colors are ethereal and have many more hues than the physical eye can discern. One can see symbols and images in the layer, as well as guides and other beings. The entire workings of the person can be viewed in the celestial body, including explosions of emotional outbursts with colors flaring, mental thoughts being processed, and physical disorders and energy manifesting. Those who are not yet working through the third eye chakra can begin to access and work with this layer through meditation and other spiritual practices.

Layer Seven: The Ketheric Body

The ketheric body extends another three to four feet around the physical body. Spiritual masters who connect with their auric bodies and fields are able to extend these fields for many more feet. These masters are also able to focus the aura, using it as a shield, and can at times physically push a person away from them using the force of the aura. Conversely, they can expand the aura and increase its magnetic energy to attract people to them.

The ketheric layer connects to the seventh (crown) chakra and, when fully open and operational, the energy emitted creates a gold and silver light. The golden light reflects during the solar time of day and the silver reflects during the lunar time of the evening. Ancients have depicted this aura and its indications of spiritual mastery by drawing or painting a golden halo around the head of spiritual masters from various cultures. This auric layer is connected to the beautiful spiritual planes that we return to once we leave the earthly plane.

How the Layers of the Aura are Affected

The etheric layer of the aura contains the energy referred to as the spirit of life. It is also referred to as the life force and is present in all living things, including plants, animals, and humans. This etheric layer works like a battery, providing energy to the body in order for it to function properly. This battery recharges itself through natural, vital energies received from the light of the sun, through energy brought in by breathing, and during the recuperative period of sleep each night.

The etheric body forms an outline of the body it surrounds and is receptive to all of the workings of the physical body, and thus is sensitive to when the body is in pain. Some photography, such as Kirlian electrophotography, has been able to detect this energy field. One noted example is a scientific experiment conducted using leaves. During the experiment, part of the leaf was torn away, yet when the photo was taken, the leaf's auric structure still existed in its totality.

When you are born, the auric shield is formed around you and operates like other natural physical functions of the body. Just as the heart knows how to beat and the body instinctively draws each breath in and out, the aura knows to expand around the body and protect you. The aura is able to recharge its energy field each night when you sleep. During your period of sleep, energy—also described as *prana* or *chi*—is restored and this allows the aura to recharge, similar to the process in which a battery receives a charge.

Delving Deeper into the Layers of the Aura

Layer One: The Etheric

As we've discussed, the first layer of the aura reflects the energy level of the person, indicating their general well-being and vitality. This layer of the aura surrounds the entire physical body in a glowing white oval shell. In its healthiest state, it is able to expand and contract with ease, allowing energy and light to move in and out from the physical body, the earthly plane, and the higher planes.

The first layer of the aura is very important, as it supports the etheric battery that generates energy and allows the restorative energy to flow from the higher layers into the physical body. When this layer is not in good shape, it slows down the flow between all of the layers. If this layer becomes too rigid, it thickens, which does not allow the energy to pass through easily. If it becomes too soft, the energy cannot be held in each layer for the appropriate amount of time needed to fully nourish the body and spirit. In addition, energy that needs to be expelled from the physical body is not able to flow easily back through the auric field. Like a clogged filter, the problem continues to worsen. The body is unable to receive the restorative energy it needs nor to expel the internal negative energy buildup.

It is rare to see a young child with a weakened first layer of the aura, as we are born with this structure firmly in place. The aura only becomes damaged over time, from high amounts of stress, emotional pain, negative thoughts, illness, and other extreme situations.

Layer Two: The Emotional

The second layer of the aura is the emotional layer and it is in this layer that most of the vivid colors can be seen. This layer changes often according to the emotions experienced by the person throughout the day. Some colors and energy remain in the aura for longer periods of time due to thoughts and energy, which are constantly being introduced to and reflected through the aura. Most people's core thoughts and beliefs remain fairly consistent, and their emotional reactions are often based upon these assessments of what they believe to be positive or negative experiences. These emotional reactions light up the emotional layer with the colorful vibrations attached to the emotions. Many psychics are able to read this layer of the aura, which reflects the potential outcome of what you are attracting into your life and thereby creating and attracting to you in your future. This is not the only level that psychics see around a person, but it is a valuable one, as you can directly change this layer with your thoughts and emotions. When doing a reading, psychics usually explain what they see around the person in these layers but that, due to the concept of free will, a person has the ability to change their thoughts and actions at any time. By doing so, they alter the outcome of the future by changing what is being directed into the energy fields. **The basic principle is: change your thinking to change your life.** What you draw to you through the principles of the law of attraction will eventually manifest in the physical plane.

Layer Three: The Mental

The third layer is the mental layer. In this layer, the colors signify the personal power colors of a person over their lifetime. This is due to the overall belief system of the person, which is held for one or several lifetimes along with karmic records and destiny. In this field, thoughts, judgments, opinions, actions, and cultural beliefs are held even more deeply than in the emotional field.

When strong positive thoughts are held in this field for a consistent period of time, the energy opens and expands to attract greater good into the field, which some people explain as being "lucky" or as having "charisma." When a high level of negative energy is held here for an extended period of time, through negative thoughts and emotions or difficult experiences that we are unable to let go of, our auric field clogs with this energy. This eventually hardens into thick clumps around the body. These blockages make it difficult for energy to pass in and out of the body. This in turn slows down the flow, creating more negative outcomes, described by some as having a "run of bad luck." Others describe this situation as having a "dark cloud over their head" and this is essentially true, since the aura itself has darkened and become clogged. This layer is directly affected by mental thoughts and by the emotions from the second layer.

When a person closes down emotionally, this layer hardens even more and creates a rough shell around the layer. In doing so, the energy sticks to the layer rather than moving freely. The result creates a wall. The longer that the second and third layer hold on to this energy, the more damage it creates around the layer. The layer eventually becomes encrusted with the energy buildup until a gritty exterior is formed. This buildup then expands into the physical body and can affect the nervous system, the organs, and the arteries (hardening). Over a period of time, this calcification in the aura even affects the facial features, giving the person a hardened look.

On the other end of the spectrum, this layer can become overwhelmed with emotional energy. When emotions run out of control for too long a period, it also affects the mental state of the person. In this situation, the layer is barely able to hold and retain its shape in the auric field. The appearance looks similar to a deflated soufflé—all the air has gone out and the crust can only do its best to maintain some form or shape. This effort has an effect on all of the auric fields, impairing the ability to move energy through this layer.

What is so powerful about the mental layer is how quickly it can change and adapt through focused energy and thought. Repeated prayers, mantras, and affirmations—all forms of focused, consistent thought reaching out to the higher planes—often can create a regeneration of the third layer.

Also important to note is that this is the layer where thought forms are created. The creation of thought forms, and how to remove them, are discussed in greater detail in chapter six.

Layer Four: The Astral

The fourth layer is the astral, which is a powerful conduit between the higher planes and the earthly plane on which our bodies are grounded. The light emitted from this level often contains rose and green colors, similar to the heart chakra. It is at the astral level that our relationships are fully defined and a connection is established energetically between two people.

THE ASTRAL LAYER IN LOVE

On this layer, energy cords are created that extend outward from our bodies in order to attach and connect with cords from other people. These cords are extremely strong and form deep connections that we take with us through lifetimes, especially with our family, children, partners, and others we love deeply. When we love someone, our astral body vibrates excitedly from this fourth layer in conjunction with the heart chakra. The phrase "to fall in love" comes from this experience. This emotion forms an energetic cord from your heart chakra in the chest, which "pulls" you to the other person. If you imagine this being a physical cord, you can see how the pulling would cause you to fall forward; thus, you fall in love. Let me explain how this beautiful energetic reaction occurs.

There is a network of smaller energy cords inside of our body, which attach to the main energy cords of the chakras and then connect to our auric bodies. In our heart chakra, we have a number of these energy cords and they are sensitive to the energy we express when we are in love. When we fall in love, an energetic vibration is created in the heart chakra area, which builds to a climactic level. This raises the energy in the heart area to the point where one of the energy cords from this area moves outward from the heart center, through the heart chakra, and engages with the auric field of the other person. It's like a jolt of love energy. The cord stays connected in this person's auric layers and seeks to connect with a similar cord extending from the other person's fourth (heart chakra) layer. When the other person experiences the same vibration of love, their cord extends and connects to the first person's cord. Once these two cords attach, the love connection is complete and the two people are united. They have formed a bond and they share energy, which passes back and forth through the attached cord.

The two people are now essentially bound together and intertwined, which is a connotation of the phrase "bound together in holy matrimony." This is why it is so difficult to disconnect from the feelings when a relationship ends, even after a bad breakup or divorce has occurred. The cord has been connected and strengthened with each experience in the union. The longer the cords have been attached, the longer it takes for them to detach and separate. Even after the cord has detached from the other person, the memory remains in the astral layer indefinitely. This also explains why the longer a couple is together, the easier it is for them to finish each other's sentences, since their cord continues to grow and expand with the connection. It is also why some people say that, over time, a married couple will begin to look alike and share some characteristics. The auric fields are blending and uniting and sharing energy on many levels.

THE ASTRAL LAYER DURING PREGNANCY

When a woman becomes pregnant, a cord from her astral layer connects with the infant to nourish it on the spiritual level. The effect is similar to the physical umbilical cord, which feeds the child inside her womb. During the first trimester, the soul of the child remains in the astral and higher planes outside of the physical body and around the mother's aura. During the first three months, the mother is aware of the child on the soul level and may dream about him or her, as the child communicates with the mother from the astral realms. As the soul of the child interacts and resides in the mother's aura, the pink hue from the astral planes around the mother intensifies, from the pure energy of the child in the astral field. This is the "glow" that many people refer to around pregnant women.

During the second trimester of pregnancy, the soul of the child descends from the higher planes and travels through the astral cord of the mother as it enters into the physical fetus inside the mother. During this trimester, the bond between mother and child is very strong and they are able to communicate with each other through the fourth layer of the aura.

By the third trimester, the glow has lessened, since the soul of the child has settled and connected inside the physical fetus. All accessible energy is being directed to the physical growth of the body, pulling energy from the outer layers of the aura inward to assist with the physical development.

When the child grows up into a young adult, the mother is reminded to "cut the cord" with the child, symbolically releasing the child to move on into adulthood. It is virtually impossible for a mother and child to truly cut this cord—they are bound so tightly and in most cases there is no need to sever their connection, with the exception of an abusive relationship, where the tie is providing negative energy. While the cord remains attached throughout the lifetime, the connection is lessened to a degree as the adult child diversifies this energy by creating new cords in new relationships of their own.

Relationship cords are formed quickly in childhood with parents, siblings, grandparents, and other close family members. This is referred to as the family ties that bind, and cord connections made in childhood are very pure and trusting. There is no hesitation on the part of children to extend cords and connect with love for others. It is only in adulthood that we tend to make a mess of these cords and create a variety of entanglements.

The experiences we have in our relationships throughout life are felt through the energy cords with each connection. The akashic records of our lives and loves can be accessed on this level, as can the connection a person has to a particular element in nature. More about both of these topics and how to access them will be discussed in chapter 9.

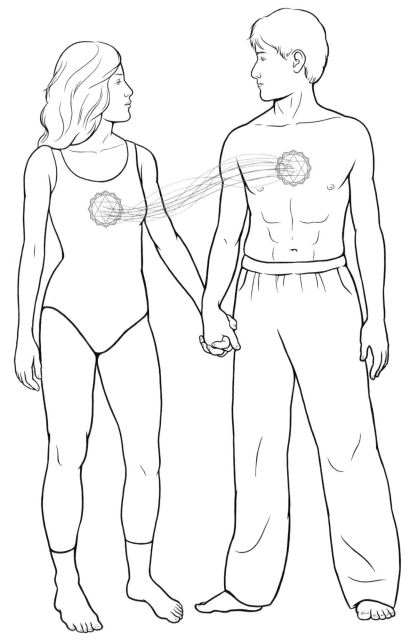

Energy cords created in the astral layer extending outward from our bodies, attaching with cords from another person. Example: "Falling in love."

Layer Five: The Etheric Template

The fifth layer is the etheric template level, which should not be confused with the etheric body of the first layer. The etheric template is a highly interactive level where the higher self can communicate between the planes and work to actively create on the body, mind, and spirit level. We interact with the higher realms and the power of the word vibrates in this layer.

In conjunction with the fifth chakra of communication, we can create magic through this auric layer. Humans are unique—we are the only beings on the earthly plane in possession of the power of speech as we know it. We are able to create sound vibrations that form into words and have the active power of expressing our will, our intent. Words have tremendous power, since they vibrate with sound and carry energy into being. When we truly understand the power of speech and the effect it has on every level, we become aware of the tremendous amount of healing or destruction we create with our words. After all, some religions believe that the entire earthly plane was created with the "Word," so just imagine what we can create every day with our words, thoughts, actions, and deeds!

Layers Six and Seven: The Celestial and Ketheric

The sixth and seventh layers are known as the celestial and ketheric levels and are rarefied layers rarely seen with the physical eye. In many cases, the energy in these levels is mainly felt or viewed through the third eye rather than seen with the physical eyes. These levels contain our higher self, our more perfected forms, which transcend from the human self and live in a state of universal love and oneness. In the current incarnation of humanity, we are in the process of refining the fourth and fifth layers of our energy bodies; some say that when we have moved into the energy bodies of the sixth and seventh layers, we will no longer even need to reside fully in our physical bodies.

As the astrological Age of Aquarius approaches, humanity is entering into a mind, body, and spirit evolutionary process in which we are evolving into superpowered beings of light. The sixth and seventh levels are engaging more in our auric bodies and I have seen over the past decade that they are altering and creating a new field around our body. As a result, our auric and etheric bodies are experiencing a transformational shift; new crystalline structures are being formed within and around the aura. These structures are creating powerful receivers that allow for enhanced psychic abilities and regenerative powers.

This auric transformation marks a historic evolution in our metaphysical bodies; we are becoming powerful light energy beings who are able to connect with the forces of the earthly plane as well as the powers from the higher planes. These changes are already being experienced and perceived by people who have a strong connection to their intuition and their energy bodies, and their understanding and acknowledgement of these changes is accelerating the process. This ties in with ancient wisdom teachings, which express that change is not only something that happens outwardly but it begins within, with what we believe is possible. More on this unique evolution in chapter 11.

Living Through the Adjustment: The Trouble with Closing Down the Fields

Because we are in a period of evolution, many people are reporting having flashes of intuition as well as paranormal and metaphysical experiences. If they are not prepared for what they encounter, it can have a negative effect on them. Being intuitive can feel overwhelming when you're constantly picking up the energy and intent from a room full of people. Also, when doing medium work and communicating with the dead, there is an energy pull from them, since they require energy to manifest and communicate on this plane. **Both activities can pull energy from a person's auric fields and deplete them if they do not take the time**

to restore themselves. As we discussed in chapter two, we are already running our auric and physical bodies at a disadvantage with poor food choices, time constraints, stress, longer working hours, and less time spent in nature and breathing in fresh air. This, combined with an intuitive or empathic person being consistently bombarded by the emotions expressed from other people, can greatly deplete the auric system. An empath does not even have to speak to the person; simply by being in their presence, their emotional field is engaged with their auric fields. This is magnified when the intuitive person is in large crowds and/or contained areas such as large buildings, malls, and concert halls. It is manageable at certain levels, but if the sensitive person does not receive enough time to release, restore, and recharge, the emotional buildup can become a real problem.

When any person grows too weary from experiencing emotions, whether from increased intuitive engagements or just a tumultuous period in daily life, they must cope. The person then can choose either a self-defensive mechanism of blocking emotions, or they can continue to drain their energy until they experience a state of depression, where their emotional body is completely exhausted. Once a person reaches either of these two states, it is difficult for the body to keep up with the demands put upon it via the emotional and mental bodies.

Both these options are counterproductive and potentially destructive to the physical person and all the auric bodies. If the emotions are blocked and trapped, additional energy is required to keep these feelings closed off, which takes away energy that would have been used for creative outlets. If the person stays overly emotional for too long, they can slip into exhaustion and depression. The emotional auric field is then damaged and unable to hold in the energy as needed. At this point, the person is like a leaking boat sinking in a turbulent sea of emotions.

Emotions are meant to be a powerful guide to lead each person to a deeper understanding while on the path of connecting with higher love through the heart chakra. The key is to understand that emotions are a valuable gift but, as with all things, we must be able to compassionately control the amount of time and energy we give to them. Like most things in life, moderation is the key. Emotions are energy, and they communicate in one form or another. Our emotional body wants to share wisdom with us, and emotions are the only form in which it is able to do this. Think of emotions as messages from your aura and you may begin to process things a little differently. It is up to each person to create a comfortable flow where they can receive and process emotions while also taking time to clear the field before receiving more emotional input and energy.

Good Circulation and Air Space

Our personal energy is also described as *chi*, a pure energy resource that is charged with positive or negative energy and the experiences that we create on a daily basis. This energy circulates around a person and creates the energy field emanating from them. This is described by some as the guiding principle of the law of attraction. The energy created in the auric field is the first thing felt by other people when you enter a room.

Thoughts and emotions have a direct effect on the energy fields surrounding each person. The energy vibration from our thoughts and emotions is stored in the mental and emotional fields. With each breath that we take, we are drawing in the emotional and mental energy we created and stored in our auric field. **With this in mind, think about your personal air space and whether or not you are creating a toxic environment with your negative thoughts and emotions.** Nobody wants to breathe in polluted air, so don't muck up the air with your own negative thoughts and unprocessed emotions.

For example, have you ever met someone for the first time and felt that this person was unhappy or angry before you even said a word to him or her? This is because their emotions are spilling forth from inside them and swirling outwardly from their energy fields. In this state, as they are releasing or fuming with anger, they are also breathing in the negatively charged air they are creating, which serves to add fuel to the fire. In this way it is easy to understand how a person can create and then get trapped in a repetitive cycle of thinking.

Another example is when a person becomes depressed for a significant period of time. As their energy lowers with the negative vibrations, their thoughts contribute to this mood. They experience a lack of energy and tend to breathe very shallowly (instead of taking deep, healthy breaths). As their negative thoughts extend outward in their aura, they breathe back in the same negatively charged energy. This continues until something is altered in the mental or emotional state that changes their frame of thinking. When this change does occur, the person might say that they have "snapped out of it" or that the "dark cloud has lifted." Someone who is feeling down because of the loss of a job or a love interest may snap out of their feelings after a few weeks because of a spark of new hope—an incredible job offer or meeting a new love interest. A person with deeper depression may require help from other sources, like a therapist, to help them review and alter their thoughts and emotions. In some cases, medication is used to alter a chemical imbalance that has been created within the body due to the downward spiral of energy to the point of depletion. A prescription, in this case, can create a barrier between the physical and emotional fields, which serves to temporarily disconnect the energy from the emotional body that created the energy that led to the depression in the first place. In these cases, medication should be combined with additional therapeutic assistance to help the person renew their awareness of hope and purpose. This provides them the energy boost needed to subconsciously recharge their mental and emotional state. It is my opinion that medication should be used only for a short period of time, as long-term use prolongs and extends the barrier between the fields.

With that said, **please defer to qualified health care professionals when considering medications and therapies for depression or other mental health issues.** Each person is unique and requires a unique approach for optimum wellness. An in-person meeting will allow your doctor or therapist to sense your aura (even if they aren't consciously doing so) and decide how to best proceed.

Depression is often described as a dark cloud or fog. For a time and age when people claim to know little about auras and energy fields, it is quite fascinating to notice how many expressions are still used that refer to these fields. A person who needs to speak with someone about a problem might say, "I need to get something off my chest," or someone in a heated argument might say, "We need to clear the air." A person who has been working too hard might say, "I need a breath of fresh air," when speaking about needing a vacation. Or when something just doesn't feel right and you can't place your finger on exactly what it is, you might say, "I'm not sure what's wrong but there's something in the air…" These are just a few examples that show how much power our auras have in our daily lives.

Hardened Auras versus Spongy Auras

Short-term unhappiness fills the aura with negative energy, but if the negativity is released soon after, the aura still maintains the same basic, healthy structure. Hardened auras are created when a person holds onto the negative energy and lives in a state of fear. A person lives in a state of fear if they believe they have no control over what is happening in their life. To counteract this fear, they attempt to control other people and situations, either from an aggressive or a passive-aggressive standpoint. Regardless of which path they take, the outcome is still the same. The aggressive tactic engages people directly with forceful and angry energy. A passive-aggressive person expends energy attempting to manipulate and guilt people into doing what they want them to do. Both options are exhausting and waste a lot of time and energy. It is also detrimental to the auric field of the fearful person, as it requires a tremendous outpouring of energy in an attempt to control every single situation. This places a great strain on the nervous system, the solar plexus, and all of the chakras. Another side effect is a low energy level, which in essence makes the person an easier target for someone wishing to harm them or dominate their energy. The auric fields are under so much pressure from having to respond to every perceived danger and stressful situation that is played over and over in the mental and emotional fields, that over time, it literally cracks under the pressure. Once the aura has cracked, it leaks energy and cannot maintain adequate energy levels. Many times this person is so obsessed with controlling situations that they don't see the real dangers coming their way. Unfortunately, because they are trapped in fear-based thinking, this only incites them to pull in further and prepare for even more dramatic situations. If this condition continues for years, the aura hardens around the body and the person also takes on a hardened appearance. This wall blocks out positive energy from easily entering their layers, which feeds their fear of life being negative. Life becomes a self-fulfilling process, as this person is actually drawing negative experiences to them with their fear and weak personal defenses.

Conversely, a person who has become severely depressed doesn't even have the energy to build up a healthy barrier around themselves. In essence, they have lost their will. The aura turns mushy and looks spongy, with holes like Swiss cheese where the energy oozes outward. The energy fields are not able to hold incoming energy for any length of time, the fields are sluggish, the chakras are overburdened, and the movement is slow. When we meet someone who has a spongy aura, we feel our energy being sucked away by this person and feel drained and exhausted after spending time in his or her presence. In a sense, they have become what is referred to as an "energy vampire." Their fields are trying to gather energy and will attempt to pull it from another person's energy field since they are unable to create it themselves. Most of the time, the person is not aware that their aura is affecting others. They are struggling and caught in a deep pit of emotion that they feel unable to climb out from. **It is not helpful to allow this person to draw upon your energy.** You may wish to help them, but feeding them your own energy will only enable their depression. The only way their auric fields can be repaired and the energy restored is by the person lifting themselves out of their mood and engaging in life again. Offer to put the person in contact with qualified health professionals and energy workers, but be sure to keep your own aura healthy and whole. Refer to chapter 7 if you need exercises to heal your own aura.

Four

IDENTIFYING COLORS IN THE AURA

First, analyze thyself. Know thyself and thy purposes. Know what ye believe, physically, mentally, spiritually. Know the sources of thy beliefs. For in such an analysis one may find self.

—Edgar Cayce

The most frequently asked question about auras has to be, "What color is my aura?" When giving an aura reading, I explain to clients that, for the most part, their aura changes color on a regular basis due to their emotions and thoughts. I also explain that there are usually one or two colors that remain consistent in their main auric field. These colors remain with the person for their lifetime unless they dramatically change their life to the point that other colors override them and change the energy resonation and vibratory energy fields.

What surprises clients the most when I read for them is that, for most of the reading, I have my eyes closed. Sometimes I have a client sit comfortably in a chair and I turn my chair and face the other way, preferring not to even look directly at them. This is because, while I can see the auric fields around each person, a person receiving an aura reading often feels uncomfortable—they become suddenly aware that, although they chose to come to me for this reading, there is a feeling of vulnerability because I am seeing who they really are. They are exposed. They begin to worry about what exactly can be seen and quietly begin asking themselves questions: "Can she read my thoughts?" If they have had a bad morning, they wonder if that energy is going to show up in their aura and they wonder if I will think less of them if I see an aura that isn't perfectly clear and shiny. In short, a reading stresses them out and this causes the aura to retract and pull in, trying to follow the instinct of the person to hide. When I relax and occasionally look the other way, it helps them to relax. It only takes a few minutes for them to get over this nervousness, as human nature has a tendency to get bored after a minute or two and their mind will wander. Once their mind wanders to another thought, the aura pops back out and is easy to read.

As a child, I saw auras around people, places, and things everywhere I went, and that was normal for me. As a teen, I was wrapped up in my own emotional auric field development and I closed down my intuitive abilities for a while, not wanting to feel and experience so much from my teen counterparts.

Later, in my twenties, I decided that I was ready to open back up my abilities and I began to practice once again seeing auras. The first few times were tense, as what came naturally to me as a child was now requiring some thought and effort on my part. Looking back, I can see how this relates to one of my favorite wisdom teachings, which is: "All that happens, happens for good." By having the natural ability to see auras in my childhood, I was able to see and experience a wide variety of auras with no judgment or barriers. Later as an adult, I had to practice to see them as fully as I had in my childhood. From this experience, I was able to understand what it was like for a person who has never seen an aura and has to practice in order to see them. This gave me great insight that I would later use when teaching others how to see auras.

As I worked to see auras at the level I saw them when I was young, something interesting occurred. I realized that the first thing I needed to do was to not try so hard; I needed to relax and allow it to come naturally. I was living in Florida in a beautiful home that had a sun porch that looked out to a canopy of trees and a waterfall running into a pond below. It was the most beautiful surrounding in which to meditate. I decided that I would begin my journey to see auras again with a practice that I enjoyed so much as a child, which was viewing the auras of trees. Each day I would spend some time on the sun porch, gazing at the trees and then seeing their auras. (I recommend this practice to anyone learning to see auras, as the trees don't mind how long you stare at them, while people often do.)

One day, as I prepared to gaze upon the auras of nature in my backyard, I closed my eyes, took a deep breath, and prepared to meditate. I had been doing this for a few moments each day to center myself before opening my eyes to see the aura of the trees. However, this time, as my eyes were closed and I centered myself and connected with the trees, I saw the auras of the trees while my eyes were still closed. This was definitely new for me! As an empathic child, I had always been sensitive to the energy fields of others without seeing them in the physical. For instance, I could feel someone approaching before they entered my room and could sense tension from people way on the other side of the house. I was used to feeling energy fields, but I had never thought to close my eyes while doing this.

With my eyes still closed, I began to see the auric fields of nature through my third eye. The auric fields were much more intense when viewed this way, and they sparkled. I saw the connections between all of nature—the leaves, the energy running through each leaf, the connection to the tree, the tree itself as it anchored into the ground, and the nourishment it received from the sunlight. Without moving my body or even turning my head, I could see my entire backyard—the energy of the water as the waterfall splashed against the rocks; the various degrees of energy being emitted from each type of plant, flower, and stone in the yard; and the movements of birds and other small animals.

This revelation began an entire new practice for me, one that I have worked to develop further in the years since that magical day. Like many experiences in life, some of the most amazing revelations come from unplanned events. Another example of this phenomenon occurred while I was reading the aura of a place rather than a living thing.

One day I was reading the aura of a home for a client. Even though I was sitting still in one room, I was traveling with my third eye to explore the entire home and assess the energy fields in each room. While I was engaged in this process, the owner's dog came into the room and sat down near me. I felt his presence, connected with it for a moment, and then turned my attention back to my work.

A few moments later, the dog heard a noise outside that alarmed him, and he barked loudly. I was so deep into my auric field scan of the house that the energy of the bark appeared in my scan. I could see the pattern of the bark and the energy being conveyed through it! It had a rhythm to it, and I realized that it made me uncomfortable on an energetic level. The dog barked several more times until the owner quieted him down.

A few minutes later, one of my client's children arrived home from school and the dog barked again, this time in an excited greeting of the newly arrived family member. This time when the dog barked, the energetic vibration in the room felt different. I realized that I was actually picking up on the energy pattern and even the intent that was being sent through the dog's bark.

When the dog barked the first time, it was a warning to a potential intruder to stay away or suffer the consequences. There is a particular frequency to this bark that can be felt energetically, which is intended to cause a reaction of fear when received in the energy fields. The second bark was an affectionate, friendly greeting and the energy released felt different. There was no sense of fear with this bark, and while the energy felt animated, it was full of excitement and joy and was completely different than the first barking situation. It was a clear example of how waves of energy communicate with sound and how we feel them first through our auric fields before processing them with our five primary senses.

These situations and many others became part of my studies over the years as I worked to gather more data on auras through my personal experiences. I realized that while seeing the colors of the auras around people was helpful, I could "see" even more with my eyes closed while looking through my third eye. Over the years, I combined my ability to see the auric fields through my physical eyes and my third eye with my empathic and psychic abilities to get a clear picture of a person when doing a reading for them. As an added bonus, over the years my spirit guides have been kind enough to jump in with information as needed as well as to help when I'm doing a consultation. (We'll explore more about spirit guides in chapter 10.)

At this point I began to experiment with sound—what it can do to the auric fields and how it can change energy. I first experimented with music, using different types of music to see and sense the vibrations from the sounds. I would experiment with how I felt after listening to a particular piece of music for a while. I would then view the aura of plants that were in the room with me, which had also been subjected to the music. I then worked with Tibetan bells to explore their range and effect, as well as wind chimes. Next I moved into working with crystal singing bowls to experience their effect on energy and the fields.

The results have been extraordinary and the side effect is that my abilities to see and sense these fields grew to an even greater capacity than I had experienced in my childhood. These practices—along with my dedication to a spiritual daily practice and the study of ancient esoteric teachings—allowed me to move into the higher spiritual planes and access information directly from the akashic records and other realms. It also enhanced my ability to communicate with spirit guides and others on the higher planes.

When I teach others about auras, they all want to begin with seeing the aura, and I understand this desire. Everyone wants to see the auric field for the first time to know that it truly exists. Each time I work with a group and a person sees an aura for the first time, it's very exciting for me; there's nothing quite like it. The feeling is similar to riding a bicycle for the first time. As soon as you let go and find that perfect balance on the bike, you never forget how to do it. I could also compare it to the old Magic Eye illusions; once you figure out the "trick" to seeing the hidden images, it's yours forever. The same goes with auras—once you learn how to relax your eyes and quiet your mind, you see the aura and you never forget how to do it again.

Having said that, like everything, you get better with practice. If you haven't been on a bike in twenty years and get back on one, you are going to be a little wobbly and unsteady. It's the same thing if you don't continue to practice seeing auras once you start viewing auras. If you don't do it often, you'll most likely only be able to see the etheric layer in a white form around the body.

Create an Aura Practice

To practice seeing auras, I instruct students to find a partner they can practice with in a comfortable space. Sit across from your partner and ask them to think of a happy moment in their lives. As they do, observe how the auric field changes and expands outward.

After a few moments, ask them to think about something they are very angry about and observe the rapid changes in the field. Continue this practice with the person thinking about different scenarios for no longer than fifteen minutes while observing the changes. I recommend a fifteen-minute limit because the person having to express all of these emotions will grow weary as they connect with various emotional states and memories. If you have a pet, they are easy to connect with and observe their aura. Ask someone else to pet them and watch how their energy field reacts to the contact. Then ask the person to engage the pet in active play and observe how the field changes again.

It has been observed that the longer two people remain together in a relationship, such as husband and wife, the more they begin to look like each other. This is because the longer two people are together in a close relationship, the more their auric fields connect and become intertwined. This is why couples are more sensitive to the feelings of each other and instinctively know and feel when the other is upset. Women in general listen more to these feelings—often referred to as "women's intuition"—and they pick up on these energy fields in their partner. They can also feel when their partner is pulling away from them and withdrawing their energy from the relationship. As the fields remain connected for years, the energy combines and some physical characteristics may grow more similar.

There is also a theory about people and their pets looking alike. More research needs to be done in this area, but there could be something to the energy radiating in the auric field of a breed of dog that creates the look and characteristics of the dog. A human who shares similar physical characteristics and similar traits may be more attracted to that breed of dog, for instance, as their energy fields harmonize better and are more aligned than with other dog breeds. This may also explain why some people are cat people and others are strictly dog people, due to the various energy vibrations and alignments between species and breeds.

What about Colors?

While explaining that it's possible to see and sense the auric fields with your eyes closed, using the third eye, I would be remiss if I didn't explain the colors you see when viewing the aura through the physical eyes. It is also important to note that colors are not the only thing you will see in an aura; there are many shapes, symbols, and imprints that also appear. We will discuss these shapes and symbols in chapter 6.

When seeing the colors of the aura, it is most important to note that a certain color can have very different meanings. The shade of the color, the clarity of the color, the hue, and even the opacity affects what the color means. It's also important to discern which colors are part of the primary colors associated with the person in this lifetime and which ones are there due to present circumstances, such as illness or a prolonged stressful period. It's best to begin by taking it all in and going over your findings. Then take a second look deeper into what is being reflected in all of the fields.

Reading the aura is more of an art than a science, as each color is presented in many hues. They can change often and need to be read overall through each layer to determine what is occurring around the person. It is also important to note that as you are connecting to your intuitive skills, some colors may appear to you in order to give you the information needed for the reading and that these colors may not necessarily be reflected in the person's aura at all times.

Included with each color listed below are recommendations on how to connect with and enhance that color, including foods, home décor, clothing, gemstones, and mantras to say while doing energy work designed to connect directly with the color in your aura and chakras.

There are two additional methods of color enhancement in general that I have found to be very effective when working with the aura.

The Power of the Sun to Restore

The first method is to drink solarized water. Pour water into a colored bottle or glass that is made of the color you desire to connect with. Set the bottle or glass in direct sunlight for an entire day. At the end of the day, the water has been infused by the energy of the sun radiating through the color of the glass. Drink the water and focus on the color as it moves through your body. This process stimulates the chakra connected with the color. Repeat the process of solarizing and drinking the water each day for one week to stimulate the associated chakra.

When doing this exercise, do not combine colors. Focus on one chakra color that you wish to enhance and restore. Along with drinking the solarized water, immerse yourself in that color and use the clothing, gemstone, and food choices listed in the color's section.

Using Indoor Lighting to Stimulate Color

The second method of color enhancement has to do with lighting. Purchase a light bulb in the color that you desire to connect with and place it in a lamp of your home. Spend an hour a day sitting near this light. Do not stare at the light bulb, as that would be harmful to your eyes and there is no need to look directly at the light. Simply sit near the light and spend some quiet time there. Meditating during this time is helpful so you can practice connecting with your energy fields and absorbing the color. If you are feeling too tired and depleted to focus on meditation, lie back and take a nap with the light on—the color will still be absorbed into your auric field.

Aura Colors and Their Meaning

Red

The color "true red" in the aura indicates physical vitality and primal power. It has a force all its own and generally indicates a strong connection with the physical body. Red is connected to the first (root) chakra.

I describe true red as appearing similar to a shiny red apple. When this color is seen in the aura, the person is very connected with their physical body. When in balance, red stimulates passion in creative and sexual forms. Those with a lot of red in their aura should take care to keep it in balance; an overabundance of red energy can lead to inflammation and circulation problems.

There is a brighter, flashier shade of red that appears in some auras and most times when I see this color it appears in people who work in very physical and exciting jobs. Examples I have seen include athletes, military personnel, firemen, and emergency medical/rescue workers who travel to a scene to help people. Oddly, I've also noted this color in horse jockeys. When I was young, my parents enjoyed going to the horse races and often would take me with them. I would watch the jockeys and the horses and noticed that when a jockey had a bright-red aura, he would often win or place high in the race. If he and the horse were in sync and their auras merged well together, the chances were even higher. If the aura of the horse was not compatible with the jockey, the red energy of the jockey would become frustrated, which diminished his connection with the horse. At that point, I knew there was little chance of the jockey winning the race, as he was not connected with his horse.

When the red color is "flaring" around the person, it looks like spaghetti sauce cooking in a pot when little bits come popping out to spatter on the stove. The red is still a shiny red, but it's bubbling. When I see this, it indicates that the person is sexually aroused and ready to engage in activity. If you want to see a lot of this red bubbling color in action, go to a nightclub. Tune in to the dance floor where people are dancing and you'll see red in the auras everywhere.

In some auras, the red color will darken and appear murky and thick. It looks more like hot lava, with a bit of black mixed in. This indicates that the person is holding on to a great deal of anger, and when they finally release that anger, it is very much like a volcanic eruption.

Typically I will also see symbols and other imprints in the aura that identify where some of the anger is based and where it originated from. This can be very helpful information if the person is willing to discuss the imprints, as we can work to let them go and release the anger in a positive manner. I always work hard to help people in these cases, since the esoteric teachings showed me that anger is a form of mental cancer; left untreated, it eats away at you from the inside out. Some people hold on to their anger, believing that it fuels and drives them and makes them feel more alive and in control. When one is ruled by anger, the emotion becomes the master and takes more energy away from the auric fields than it gives back. The result is that the person becomes drained and depleted. The only emotion they can pull from their surroundings is the anger, which becomes a self-defeating process as it takes even more energy to pull up and release the anger. The process is similar to what it feels like when the adrenal glands are depleted.

RECOMMENDATIONS TO CONNECT WITH AND ENHANCE RED

Foods: Red apples, cherries, tomato sauce, beets, red peppers, tomatoes, tomato juice, strawberries, and red kidney beans.

Home Décor: A fire in the fireplace or from candlelight is the easiest way to connect with the energy of red in your home, and this can be taken a step further by using a red candle. Red paint can feel aggressive and should be used sparingly in the home. The best room for red in the home is the dining room, where the warmth is presented with food and only brief periods of time are spent in the room for this activity. An all-red kitchen would be overwhelming and out of balance, but punches of red in the kitchen in accent areas, such as a backsplash, provides the same warmth as created in the dining room. Typically, I recommend not using red in the bedroom. Some people think of using this color to ignite passion, but most times it just interferes with getting a restful night's sleep and radiates too much fire energy, which stimulates arguments instead of healthy passions.

Clothing: A punch of red worn around the neck, such as a scarf for women or a tie for men, increases your forcefulness and power. A red shirt or dress exudes sensuality, physical activity, and drive. Wearing red pants or a skirt typically brings the energy down and reduces the energy flow and thus should be avoided. The one exception is red shoes—these indicate a smoldering sexuality and burning passion and will ignite sexual fire.

Gemstones: Red jasper, hematite, ruby, garnet, obsidian, red carnelian, and red coral.

Flowers: Red roses, hibiscus, geraniums, red azalea, peonies, red tulips, red salvia, red amaranth, poinsettia, Christmas cactus, red crocus, gladiola, anthuriums, and amaryllis.

Music: Tribal music, such as drumming, and the flute are good to soothe and connect with the energy of red and the root chakra.

Activities: Spending time in nature is very nurturing for red energy. If there is an overabundance of red energy, a strenuous activity like hiking will help to release the energy through the physical exercise. Afterward, spend time in a sauna to sweat out toxins and release old energy. To connect and balance with red energy, get your hands in the earth. Gardening and planting will restore and connect your body and all of the energy fields with your root chakra, grounding you again into your center.

Mantra: *I am safe and protected. All is well in my world. I am grounded by Earth and filled with light and power. Change is the natural order of the world and whatever changes I face, I am strong and handle them easily and comfortably.*

Orange

Orange is the color of joy and opening to spiritual consciousness. It is no surprise to me to find that many orders of monks wear orange robes. I've also noticed that children love the color orange and will use it often when coloring pictures. They also enjoy wearing the color and many will be drawn to orange and purple colors when given a choice, which are very complimentary for the energy fields. Orange is warm and vibrant and indicates that the person is receiving new information and energy from the other planes. Orange is an infusion of energy. A person with an orange aura will generally be outgoing in nature, have inspirational things to say, and will do well in public speaking and working with groups of people.

In my work, it has been rare for me to see someone with orange as the main aura color where it wasn't bright and shiny. I have seen the color orange appear in one section of the aura where it was dull and muddy, but never in the full intensity of the aura. When I see orange that has become dark and muddy, it indicates that the person is cranky and irritable and definitely not in a creative mood. This color seems to come and go in the emotional field, and it rarely stays in this hue for long. If the person goes through a longer period of feeling irritable, the aura seems to move into an angry red.

Interestingly, as children grow into adults, they seem to pull away from the color orange. I've often mused that as kids have to spend more time in the mundane realities of the earthly plane, they lose some of the connection with the pure joy of learning and opening to new information. Their guard comes up as a protective measure, and this slows the connection to orange energy. As adults, we can recapture this energy to help open ourselves up to the energy of orange. Most of us have a difficult time wearing the color orange, so the next best thing is to eat one. As you enjoy an orange at breakfast, savor the taste and the juice and invite the energy from the orange to infuse its essence into your energetic fields.

Recommendations to Connect with and Enhance Orange

Foods: Oranges, carrots, mangos, clementines, passion fruit, cinnamon, paprika, cantaloupe, pumpkin, and apricots.

Home Décor: Orange is wonderful in the home and is best used in colorful accents like pillows and candles. A little orange is all you need to wake up the energy in the room and create a strong vibe. Children may ask to have their room painted orange, but it can prove to be too stimulating for them. Instead, supplement orange in a bedspread, pillows, curtains, or other accent pieces. Orange as a wall color is not recommended, even in the dining room. It creates an energy vibration to hurry, and that is not suitable when dining and attempting to digest properly. Many fast food restaurants use a combination of red and orange in their décor to encourage their customers to eat quickly and leave, making room for more customers to have seating. While this is effective in that regard, it is not the desired outcome I would choose when dining at home.

To recharge the energy in the home, rather than using an orange light bulb in a lamp, I recommend using a Himalayan salt lamp, which gives off a beautiful orange glow.

Clothing: Wrap yourself in an orange robe to infuse the body with the creative juiciness of orange. There's really not a bad way to wear orange, so cover yourself in it from head to toe when you feel the need to connect with orange. On occasions when this is not a good fashion choice, an orange scarf will work nicely.

Gemstones: Garnet, amber, orange calcite, orange carnelian, orange aventurine, orange garnet, tiger's eye, and sunstone.

Flowers: Orange daylily, lantana, orange tulips, bird of paradise, oriental poppy, orange zinnia, peach tulips, orange Gerber daisies, gladiolas, Echinacea "Harvest Moon," and orange blossoms.

Music: Chanting by monks, classical music of Vedic origin, Indian folk music, and the blowing of the conch shell as done in Hawaii.

Activities: Connecting in the water is the best way to stimulate and revive orange energy. Spend time near the ocean, swimming and exercising in a pool, and near waterfalls. Massage is especially helpful to stimulate and circulate orange energy as well as soothe the second chakra. Lymphatic massage is especially therapeutic for this color.

Mantra: *I connect to who I am at my deepest level. I acknowledge my feelings and understand that they are here to teach me more about myself. I will no longer hide from my feelings; I embrace them and welcome the journey. I live in joy and find happiness and peace in each day.*

Yellow

Yellow seen in the aura typically indicates a high intellect and connection to the third (solar plexus) chakra. The person with a strong yellow presence is typically an academic type or inventor who expends most of their energy in their mental field. They are passionate about concepts and ideas and are driven by achieving results and making discoveries rather than by earning financial rewards. Money is just the means to allow them to do the work they are passionate about. They are often drawn to rooms painted yellow in color, which further stimulates their mental state.

Yellow in the aura indicates that the person is open to learning more about whatever is being discussed or presented. As long as yellow is seen as a clear bright hue, it generally is a positive sign to do with the mental energy fields working in order and assimilating information. Classrooms would function well if painted in a soft, warm yellow, inviting the mental energy field to pay attention and open to the information presented.

When yellow becomes dull in color, it represents a lack of interest and that the person is withdrawing from their intellectual self and wallowing in a lazy way. When yellow becomes darker yet, the person is in a state of ego and has closed off to accepting new information or changing their mind. They are convinced that what they know is best and do not wish to receive any information to the contrary.

Unfortunately this color can be seen too often in academics, professors, scientists, and religious zealots who are building up walls of resistance to any information that differs from their beliefs. This usually occurs when the person feels that their opinions are not being accepted or taken seriously. It manifests first as a lack of self-esteem or self-confidence. The result is to build a wall of self-righteousness in order to regain a sense of confidence and control.

When yellow has a greenish hue to it, the mental field is sluggish and overtaxed. This color generally indicates the person has lost interest in being creative and is moving to a negative state filled with jealousy, dishonesty, and greed.

RECOMMENDATIONS TO CONNECT WITH AND ENHANCE YELLOW

Foods: Lemons, sunflower seeds, dairy products, cumin, corn, egg yolks, yellow peppers, pasta, and grains. When needing to calm the third chakra area, mint, ginger, and chamomile tea are especially helpful.

Home Décor: A warm, sunny yellow is a welcome addition in any home, and rooms best suited to this color would include a sunroom or family room. In this particular case, yellow is best energized in the home through paint rather than in lighting or decorative accents. The only exceptions are an arrangement of fresh flowers in yellow or a large bowl of yellow lemons in the kitchen.

Clothing: Pale yellow is a good color to wear, especially in a shirt or cardigan. Bright yellow tends to be too stimulating to wear on the body. Yellow jewelry is a better choice in the bright color hue.

Gemstones: Yellow citrine, yellow diamond, lemon quartz, and yellow topaz. Many of the gemstones from the orange family are also helpful with yellow energy, including amber and tiger's eye.

Flowers: Daisies, yellow daylilies, yellow roses, yellow tulips, mums, black-eyed Susans, daffodils, yellow irises, yellow archangels, marigolds, witch hazel, forsythia, and buttercups.

Music: Calming classical music of any style.

Activities: Spending quiet time in the sunshine, such as lounging in a chair outside while reading a good book. Stimulate the mind by engaging in crossword puzzles, reading, and conversing with others. Expand the mind by taking a course on something that is completely new to you.

Mantra: *My opinion matters and it is communicated confidently and with ease. I am confident in expressing my ideas and share them openly with others in warm and engaging conversation. My ideas are understood and held in regard by others. I understand that each person is entitled to their own personal beliefs and ideas. I respect these beliefs and ideas and welcome the opportunity to learn more about them and myself through a respectful exchange.*

Green

The color green in the aura reflects many of the qualities found in trees. Green is calm, restorative, and abundant. When a person maintains a consistent green auric energy field, they exude a healing energy. In return, they are nurtured and healed themselves by spending time in nature. People with a primary green aura are loving, kind, and compassionate and require frequent periods of private time to recharge their energy because they give so abundantly to others.

When green is seen predominately in the aura, it indicates that the person is opening and operating from the fourth (heart) chakra level. People with this energy are warm, friendly, and welcoming. Many empaths radiate with green energy from the heart area, along with pink, both of which are connected to this chakra. If you are drawn to pink and green, there's a good chance that you are working on opening your heart chakra. Your higher self is connecting you to these colors and wants them around your energy field.

When green appears dark or muddy, it indicates jealousy, spite, and envy. If the green has a yellow tinge to it, the person has overloaded their mental energy field to the point of exhaustion and will not be making clear decisions. Because of this imbalance, it is easy for them to feel jealous or envious of others. They feel depleted and overloaded and the emotions soon turn to feelings of resentment and anger. The phrase "green with envy" is a good example of how this color washes over a person, reflecting the mental and emotional fields around them. I once knew a woman whose aura was almost completely covered in this sickly green color. I only saw her once a year or so, and each time the green had expanded. The last time I saw her, the sickly green had expanded to the point where her physical skin had a greenish-yellow tinge to it and her eyes appeared to have narrowed. My first thought was that she was beginning to look like a reptile. Reptiles are cold-blooded with a tough skin; this woman gave off that same appearance and energy. She had pulled away from the warmth of her heart chakra and was creating a tough skin around herself filled with her jealousy, envy, and spite.

Dark green can symbolize a person who is overly focused on money, to the point of greed taking over rational thought. I've been in corporate buildings where the focus has been maintained for years on profit and greed, and the building itself resonates with that clouded aura. When you see this color green around a person, be very careful. If you can, avoid doing business with them, for their "heart" truly is in the wrong place when it comes to money matters.

RECOMMENDATIONS TO CONNECT WITH AND ENHANCE GREEN

Foods: All green vegetables and fruit including spinach, kale, green peppers, limes, broccoli, celery, green tea, lettuce, parsley, and cabbage.

Home Décor: Green is a soothing color in any room of your home and can be used in almost any design of your choosing. Paint the walls green, use green accents and accessories—there's no limit! I had an emerald green sofa that students sat on for years while studying wisdom teachings with me. They enjoyed sinking into it and they found it to be warm, inviting, and soothing. Almost everyone had a comment and memory to share with me about the sofa when it had finally run its course and was ready to be retired.

Pale green, dark green, and emerald green are all soothing to almost every energy field. The only green to shy away from when decorating is an overabundance of a yellowish green. Too much of this color in the home can have a draining effect on the aura, but is fine used in small doses. Green plants are a wonderful addition to the home, softening the energy and providing a welcoming touch.

Clothing: There's a right shade of green for any skin tone, so try on several colors and ask a friend to help see which one looks best with your skin and hair coloring. Most times, the color green that looks best on your physical body is also the one that is the right choice for your auric field. As the axiom states: "As Within, So Without." We manifest internally and outwardly in a harmonic vibration of who we are and what colors we resonate with.

Gemstones: Emerald, malachite, rose quartz, jade, and tourmaline.

Flowers: Green plants of any variety and shape. See also the flowers listed for pink, as pink flowers enhance the green auric field.

Music: Metaphysical music that lifts energy, especially when it features the sounds of the ocean, including dolphins and whales. Traditional folk music from all cultures is well received. Celtic music is especially good to connect with green.

Activities: Connecting with others in loving and accepting ways. Meditations to open the heart chakra are very helpful. Engaging in active practices of nonjudgment, compassion, and sensitivity toward others will speed and enhance opening this energy field and chakra.

Energy work and massage are very beneficial in opening this field as well. Spending time at the beach, where the ocean waves hit the sand, can be helpful in healing and opening the heart chakra.

Mantra: *I am love. I forgive all transgressions presented to me and I live in a sea of unconditional love. All is well in my world and each action I take is for my highest and best good. I love myself and accept myself as the pure divine being that I am. I give thanks and know that divine energy is flowing through me, healing and replenishing me in every way.*

Blue

Blue, the color of the ocean and the sky, is by far the most popular color in the world. Most people find some form of blue to be relaxing. Blue in the aura reflects generally the same intention—a person who is calm, relaxed, interested in their work, and generally well balanced in life. They have a deep interest in their spiritual path and are honest and forthcoming. The phrase "true blue" is a reflection of the personality found in a person with a primarily blue aura. If a streak of bright blue is seen in the aura, it generally indicates that the person is receiving or sending energy and communication from the intuitive planes.

Deeper blue shows a connection with the yellow mental field of thought. The blue harmonizes with the mental field and enables the person to work in an orderly fashion in order to accomplish their goals. A brighter, incandescent blue symbolizes that the person is open and connecting intuitively and is receiving information from the Other Side, possibly in direct downloads of information. When seen with a mixture of white light, this blue indicates the presence of a spirit guide or other being communicating with the person.

Often a person is not yet aware that they are opening their intuitive side, and so the information will just appear to them in their thoughts as an inspirational moment or idea. When they are asked how they came up with the answer, they are unsure and might say that the answer came to them "out of the blue." Without realizing it, they are accurately describing the auric field color around them, where their mental energy field connected with their intuitive abilities to draw the energy down into the aura, bringing the information to them.

When bright, clear blue is in the aura, the fifth (throat) chakra is fully activated and the person is able to communicate and speak their ideas and feelings effectively and clearly. This type of communication is well received by others and the speaker sounds and feels dynamic and engaging.

When a muddy dark blue is seen in the aura (think of mixing black and blue together), it indicates a person is withdrawn and blocked. They have overloaded their fields to the point where they are losing their clear connection to the mental fields and are running out of ideas. This leads to panic in the emotional field and a need for control, as the sense of control is slipping away from their grasp. Because the channel is so blocked, it is not easy to access information from the mental field and they have difficulty retaining and remembering information, which only stresses them further. The best thing a person can do when their aura is overwhelmed with this dark, blue-black color is to take a vacation and allow some time for the systems to clear and come back into balance. They are overworked and need time to rest and recuperate. Once the person recovers, they will need to communicate to others what has been bothering them and be heard and acknowledged.

Blue often becomes blocked because people do not share their feelings or they keep them bottled up inside. If they do not balance the blue energy in their field, they either don't share their feelings at all or they talk too much but nothing they say is taken seriously since they are rambling on and on. They talk in circles, never really getting to what they are feeling inside, and this only makes them feel worse and causes others to pull away.

One very negative side effect is that the muddy blue person will turn to gossip, either directly with other people or escaping with celebrity gossip reports. They do this in order to feel better by comparing themselves in this manner rather than focusing on stating their true feelings and establishing a deeper communication with others. They have become paralyzed in fear and are afraid that others will not like them if they reveal who they truly are. They become lost in an endless sea of blue.

Recommendations to Connect With and Balance Blue

Foods: Blueberries and plums. Liquids are most important when clearing and balancing blue energy, including water and herbal teas with lemon and honey. Pure natural fruit juices are also beneficial.

Home Décor: Blue works in any form and fashion in the home, whether in paint colors, floor colors, drapes, furniture, or accessories. Avoid too much navy or dark blue on the walls, though, as it can close in the energy and cause it to stagnate. I have seen some rooms where navy on the walls can work, but it has to be carefully balanced with lots of windows, golden oak hardwood, or light tile floors and other accents to catch the light and circulate the energy around the room. The effect of a dark blue room can be striking, but it requires more effort to keep the energy moving.

Clothing: A navy blue suit subliminally communicates that a person is confident, dependable, capable, and honest. I'd recommend it any time for a job interview. There is a shade of blue that looks good on every person. Try them all and see what feels best for you, and don't be surprised if it changes over time as your aura develops!

Gemstones: Lapis, topaz blue, aquamarine, and calcite blue.

Flowers: Blue iris, hyacinths, delphiniums, and forget-me-nots.

Music: Jazz, the blues (naturally), pop, and rock.

Activities: Sailing, cruising, any activity in the water, singing, karaoke, participating in a choir, and attending or taking part in theater, musicals, and plays.

Mantra: *I trust that my words are clear and spoken with true intent. When I speak, others hear and acknowledge my thoughts and words and receive them with ease. I am dignified and intelligent and trust that there is a divine plan taking place at this time. My thoughts are clear, my mind is open to receive, and beneficial information is coming to me every day to guide me in my work.*

✧

Secondary Colors

Red, orange, yellow, green, and blue are the most common colors seen in the aura. The following colors are not as predominant as the colors already discussed. They are most often seen periodically, such as when a person is experiencing a strong emotion like love, when a person has become depressed, or if a person is experiencing a spiritual connection and awakening.

Purple

Purple, violet, or lavender in the aura is such a lovely sight to see. In most cases, this person is connecting with the spiritual realms and building on their intuition and spiritual connection. It is one of the highest levels of auric vibrations in the human aura. It is assumed that if someone is psychic, they are receiving energy through their sixth (third eye) chakra. While this is accurate, there is more here than meets the "eye," literally. Each chakra and energy field builds upon the next, beginning with the first chakra and continuing up the spine of the body until it reaches the sixth chakra. When the portals of each chakra have opened enough to raise energy to the sixth chakra, the effect is the ability to "see" beyond the Veil and receive information flowing from the higher planes.

What is not often discussed is that there is a great variety in how open this area can be, and the level of energy clarity in this area determines how much information comes into the energy field to be received.

People with psychic ability do not have to be spiritual in order to obtain information, but people who work to embrace their spiritual bodies as well as their intuitive field are often able to receive information from higher planes.

Energy is always present and flowing, but the difference between a spiritual psychic and a nonspiritual one is like a water faucet that opens only just a bit to receive a trickle and a faucet that is able to turn on full blast and receive an enormous flow of water. There is a built-in protective system in our psychic selves that first allows the energy to only trickle in, so that the psychic can become comfortable with accessing the information from the closest planes and the initial insights are not overwhelming to receive. As the psychic develops further and works on their spiritual connection, the flow continues to expand into the higher realms, so that they can become comfortable with the expanded flow of information. Opening the floodgates right away would be overwhelming and a shock to the system.

It is rare to see a person with a primary indigo, violet, or purple aura. When you do, the person is usually a visionary with a deep sense of service to humanity. More often, one sees flashes of violet and purple in the aura, which constitute a flow of energy when the person is doing psychic work or in a deep spiritual state of ecstasy and connection with the Divine.

There is a poem written by Jenny Joseph in 1961 entitled "Warning: When I Am an Old Woman." In the poem, she states, "When I am an old woman, I shall wear purple." I'd like to think that Ms. Joseph was connecting with her sixth chakra purple energy and, in her own way, is writing about what I refer to as "Wise Woman wisdom"—the deep intuitive knowledge and wisdom that every woman carries inside of her. As women enter into their 50s, they begin the Wise Woman cycle and the purple energy expands greater in their energy fields. Wearing purple is one way to connect with the energy and allow it to expand.

When purple becomes muddy, the person is out of balance and has spent too much time pushing their way into the other realms without having a clear channel in the energy fields to do so. Because they are forcing the experiences, the lower bodies become gray and this mixes in with the purple, causing a muddied effect. They experience very uncomfortable side effects when pushing to open this field, including encounters with lower level beings from the Other Side and having troubling nightmares. Pushing this energy field open when one is not ready breaks the protective shield that is normally in place. This field is ready to open and close naturally as the energy raises and lowers. When it is pushed open, it shatters the field and the person becomes overly sensitive, out of balance, and loses some touch with reality. They may hallucinate and become overwhelmed, picking up on every little energy imprint from every person around them. With no balance to discern what they are feeling, they are overwhelmed and crippled in their mental and emotional fields. It is best to allow this process to open naturally, which will happen if one works to balance the lower fields and chakras first.

RECOMMENDATIONS TO CONNECT WITH AND BALANCE PURPLE

Foods: When entering the higher energetic levels and sixth (third eye) and seventh (crown) chakras, food does not have the same effect on these light bodies. Grapes and grape juice may be beneficial to balance at times. To ground the body after psychic work, dark chocolate is recommended to connect to center.

Home Décor: Purple in the home works best in small doses. I love purple and have incorporated it in my home in various ways, including purple drapes. For years, I used an eggplant purple chair exclusively for meditation and psychic work. Purple pillows, bedspreads, and accents work best to bring this energy into the home.

Clothing: Wearing purple connects one with the feeling of royalty and divinity. When feeling bold, people are drawn to wearing purple for a specific event. Most times, though, it is more welcoming and energy-enhancing to wear it in the lighter form of lavender. Lavender is the softer side of purple and is calming, graceful, and intuitive. Use lavender colors in the home and in your clothing to enhance this energy without overwhelming yourself or others.

Gemstones: Amethyst, tanzanite, purple topaz, moonstone, purple fluorite, clear quartz, and diamond.

Flowers: Violets, purple aster, lavender, larkspur, hydrangea, monkshood, evening primrose, Scottish thistle, purple sage, lilacs, and purple tuberose.

Music: At this level, each person has to find and connect with the music that personally lifts their spirit and touches their soul. There is no one type of music that works here. Working with crystal singing bowls is very helpful.

Activities: Guided meditations that help you visualize, study with teachers on metaphysical topics, and energy work. Pay attention to your dreams, keep a journal, engage in service work, and practice giving without thought of compensation. Spend time outdoors in the evening enjoying the moon and stars.

Mantra: *I am one with the Universe. I am open to receiving the bountiful gifts that are mine by divine right and for my highest and best purpose. In return, I pledge to be in service to humanity, to assist others, and to think of others with unconditional love and compassion. I accept the truth about who I am as well as who each person is, both in their gifts and in their shortcomings. I release my past, my fears, and my old patterns of negative thinking. I replace them with love, light, and positive affirmations. Each day I am growing stronger in the light and wiser in the ways of the ancients.*

White

White is the color seen around the first (etheric) layer of the aura. When a person first begins to see the auric field around the body, this is what they see—the glowing white light that radiates around the physical body. This white light reflects the life force radiating from the spirit and the auric energy fields. Still, white is rarely seen as the primary color in the overall aura, and once a person has more practice in seeing the aura, the colors surrounding the auric fields quickly predominate and are more vivid and exciting than the white glow of the first etheric field.

When white is seen swirling in patterns around the aura, it indicates the person is speaking truthfully and clearly about the topic. Orbs of white light that are focused in a ball or spiral shape indicate spiritual beings in the energy fields surrounding the person; they may be attempting to communicate with the person.

When the protective shield of the aura is enlarged and expands outward to protect the physical body, it glows with a white light and appears like a bubble of white light around the person. This can be extended outward from the person to protect other fields around them, including people, animals, buildings, and vehicles.

RECOMMENDATIONS TO CONNECT WITH AND BALANCE WHITE

Foods: Most foods are not meant to assist with raising the white light energy around you. When you are preparing to work with raising your energy, it's better to do so on an empty stomach.

Home Décor: White works in all capacities and styles. The main thing to focus on is whether there is an underlying tone of blue or yellow to the white. The subtle hue difference can make a big energy impact, causing the room to feel cool, calm, and peaceful with blue hues or warm and inviting with yellow.

Clothing: White clothing also works in all variety of styles. When doing energy work and seeking to connect with the higher realms, wear white that is of a natural fiber, such as cotton or silk. Avoid wearing manmade synthetic fabrics, as they interfere with the auric energy fields.

Gemstones: Moonstone, clear quartz, opal, pearls, diamond, drusy quartz, and ammonite.

Flowers: White roses, white daffodils, white amaryllis, magnolia, clematis, honeysuckle, mountain laurel, white lilacs, sweet peas, white tulips, gladiolas, tuberose, bunny tails, white zinnia, calla lily, white carnation, white petunia, white poinsettia, white geraniums, white asters, dogwood, lily of the valley, and orchids.

Music: Uplifting music that relaxes and calms the spirit.

Activities: Take three deep breaths, breathing in slowly and pulling in fresh clean air. When breathing out, blow out forcefully, releasing the stagnant air from inside. Each time you breathe in, visualize the pure, cleansing air coming into your body and auric field. Each time you breathe out, visualize all stagnant and negative energy leaving your body and clearing from your auric field. After taking the three deep breaths, visualize the aura around your body being filled with beautiful white light. See the light and help it to expand around the oval shape of your aura. Picture your body and your auric fields glowing with pure white light, filled and operating at full capacity.

Mantra: *I am filled with the Pure White Light. Nothing but Good can come to me, nothing but Good shall come from me. I give thanks. I ask for Divine Order, Divine Wisdom, and Divine Guidance. (Repeat three times.)*

Gold

When gold is seen in the aura, it indicates spiritual mastery and a connection with ascended beings on the higher planes. This was often portrayed in paintings of spiritual masters and enlightened spiritual teachers who were depicted with gold halos around their head, representing their golden aura and spiritual enlightenment.

Gold in the aura is overwhelmingly positive and also indicates wisdom and generosity. I have never seen gold in an aura where it did not represent that something beautiful was taking place for the person. The color gold in the aura is most commonly seen around the head and the heart chakra area. When an abundance of gold is found in the aura, the person radiates and glows with the gold energy, becoming like the sun. Spiritual masters who achieve this level of enlightenment see their auras fully restored and they are able to radiate energy to others in healing capacities.

There are some occasions when the gold color appears muddy in the aura. When this is seen, it represents that the person is in the process of alchemically transmuting the lower level energy out of their aura, in order to turn it to gold. The lingering colors are being burned away from the auric fields, muddying the energy field as they burn and are removed. This is a temporary refining process as the person continues on their enlightened journey. Truly, like the old saying, when you see this color in the aura, the person is "as good as gold."

RECOMMENDATIONS TO CONNECT WITH AND ENHANCE GOLD

Foods: Herbal teas and eating light meals four or five times a day, rather than three heavy meals, helps with the transmutation. Ginger ale is also helpful.

Home Décor: Gold is a beautiful accent to use in the home in all forms of décor, especially when blended with white.

Clothing: Gold is best represented in the metal form, such as in jewelry, rather than being worn as clothing.

Gemstones: Gold.

Flowers: Plumeria, gold poppy, buttercups, lantana "Gold Mound," achillea "Coronation Gold," and Bidens "Gold Spark."

Music: Like the higher level auric fields and chakras, music can only serve at this level to lift the spirit, so choose what feels right to you. Crystal singing bowls, chants, and Tibetan bells are also helpful.

Activities: The transmutation to gold in the aura happens when the other aura fields and chakras are clear and aligned and the person is engaged in deep spiritual work. There is no short-cut to the auric fields attuning to the gold color in the aura—it is an alchemical transmutation from the lower bodies into the higher bodies.

Mantra: *Hear me now, O Divine One, spirit of all and keeper of wisdom. I see you and now you see me and we are one. Gather unto me with your wisdom and keep me safe as I journey deep into the realms of my soul. My step is sure and my burden light as I transmute my energy from light into gold.*

Silver

Silver is rarely seen as a true full color in the aura. It is usually seen in streaks or sparkles around a person. Ted Andrews, in his book *How to See and Read the Aura,* gives one of the best examples I have ever encountered of what these silver sparkles look like. He calls them "twinklies." He reports that twinklies appear in auras, especially in women who are about to become pregnant or are pregnant. If he saw twinklies around a woman and she was not pregnant, he would caution her that there was that type of energy around her and if she were not ready to have a child, she would need to take extra precautions.

When I see silver in the aura, I describe it as sparkles. I sometimes see silver in long streaks around the aura. It usually indicates that something magical or miraculous is occurring around the person. I have never seen silver as the primary aura color in a person.

What I have seen most often with silver is a beautiful sheen around some women and men who understand and work with the forces of magic. Silver seems to only appear in the aura for a period of time, to bring creative energy and life-force energies, such as a pregnancy, or to manifest something that requires a great deal of creative force, such as seen in magical workings. I've observed silver in the aura during high magical activities such as a high priestess conducts in rituals. When one engages in rituals and spells, such as drawing down the moon, silver also appears in the auric fields.

RECOMMENDATIONS TO CONNECT WITH AND ENHANCE SILVER

Foods: Not applicable.

Home Décor: I've noticed with great interest the current trend toward metallic and stainless-steel appliances in the home. Perhaps this will stimulate the creative energy and force needed to turn the current economy around, by stimulating this energy in the home. Using real silver, though, is the best way to connect with the energy of silver. Though they were once common, it is rare to find silver utensils and teapots used in the home these days, due to the time required for care and polishing. Your best choice may be to purchase a silver coin.

Clothing: Silver, like gold, is better worn as jewelry than as clothing.

Gemstones: Silver, moonstone, clear quartz, and pearl.

Flowers: A branch from a weeping willow tree or a rowan tree, and white sage.

Music: Like the higher level auric fields and chakras, music can only serve at this level to lift the spirit, so choose what feels right to you. Crystal singing bowls, silver bells, and chimes connect with the appropriate energy.

Activities: Spending time in the moonlight and starlight will connect you with the energy of silver. Magical activities done in the moonlight will attract silver energy as well.

Mantra: *By the light of this moon, I embrace you, Divine Mother. Protect me, guide me, and hold me in your arms as I embark on this creative endeavor. I am yours and where there is water, I hear your name. Where there is a breeze, I feel your embrace, and where there is love, there is life. Be with me now as I travel on this path and seek the knowledge of the muses to assist me. Guide me and comfort me in my time of need. In your name, I give thanks.*

Pink

Pink in its clearest form in the aura represents joy, romantic love, and an optimistic view of the world. When pink is mixed with a bit of orange, it has reached its highest level, mixing the second (sacral) chakra into the higher forms of love of the fourth (heart) chakra, representing balance between the physical, emotional, and spiritual forms of love. Pink in warm shades flaring around the aura indicates the person is in the process of falling in love.

A washed-out and faded pink or a muddy pink aura represents a person who has not developed fully from their childhood. They are struggling with immaturity and are uncertain in matters of love and relationships. They often struggle with codependency and feelings of helplessness.

Pink is rarely seen as a predominant color in the aura for extended periods of time. The most common examples of seeing pink in the aura include the first trimester of pregnancy, when a person is falling deeply into romantic love, and around newborn babies. Attracting pink into the aura can assist with healing the emotional and physical body, especially to do with the heart.

RECOMMENDATIONS TO CONNECT WITH AND ENHANCE PINK

Foods: Sherbet, pink grapefruit, pink lemonade, and watermelon.

Home Décor: Light pink in the home works best in a young girl's room. Bolder shades of pink, including fuchsia, make wonderful compliments against deeper jewel tones, such as sapphire blue and emerald green.

Clothing: Wear fuchsia pink to express confidence and passion. Light pink is soft and inviting and expresses a gentle, artistic soul.

Gemstones: Rose quartz.

Flowers: Pink roses, hibiscus, pink alstroemeria, pink lilies, pink Gerber daisies, "Stargazer" lilies, pink carnations, pink orchid, wild basil, pink lady's slipper.

Music: To connect with pink energy, listen to the old swing song by Glenn Miller titled "In the Mood."

Activities: Falling in love will turn your aura pink in a heartbeat (pun intended). Learning to love yourself first will keep pink in your aura for the long-term.

Mantra: *I am filled with love. I glow with loving energy and love myself inwardly and outwardly. Everything I see is through the eyes of love and that love is reflected back to me. I am in the pink and see the world through my new shade of rose-colored glasses.*

Turquoise

Many references about the color turquoise in the aura are included in the description of blue. I decided to give turquoise its own classification as a color in the aura, due to the evolutionary changes I have been observing in the auric fields over the past decade.

I am now seeing more people with a primary color of turquoise in their aura, and it is noticeably different than the darker teal color that used to appear with the blue in the aura. This turquoise color is one that was very predominant during the time of ancient Egypt and is returning again in many auras. People with a predominant amount of turquoise in their aura are old souls who are bringing back with them their knowledge of the ancient ways, especially knowledge to do with ancient healing techniques. Turquoise in the aura represents natural leaders with a strong desire to share their vision, and these people are naturally drawn to teach, heal, and inspire.

When turquoise appears muddy or murky, the person is struggling between what they have been told they must do in this lifetime and what they are feeling on the soul level that they are truly here to accomplish.

Recommendations to Connect with and Enhance Turquoise

Foods: Not applicable.

Home Décor: Turquoise in the home raises the vibrational energy of a person working to connect with their ancient wisdom. Natural elements such as turquoise-colored tiles are helpful, as is living near water or the presence of running water near the home, such as from a swimming pool or fountain.

Clothing: Turquoise-colored clothing.

Gemstones: Turquoise, moonstone, lapis, and copper.

Flowers: Orchids from Hawaii. Also organics like seashells and starfish.

Music: Instruments with strings, such as the guitar and the violin.

Activities: Try taking courses in ancient esoteric teachings and holistic healing, reading books on these topics, and traveling, especially to foreign countries and the sea.

Mantra: *Hear me now, O ancient ones. I hear your call and stand ready to return to service. I am surrounded by pure white light and ask that only that which is for my highest good is presented to me now, so that I may connect to the path formed by my ancestors. I return here and now to carry on what was begun ages ago, to bring it to fruition. As it once was, so it shall be again.*

Gray

Gray in the aura symbolizes depression, the upcoming manifestation of an illness, or a clouded aura that may soon result in either of these situations. When the aura is gray, the person is unable to clear their energy and requires help to move the energy out. Seeking the assistance of an energy worker to clear the aura will help in that moment, but the problem will soon return unless the person is helped to release what is causing their sadness in the mental and emotional fields.

A gray aura is typically damaged and leaking energy and the entire auric field will need repair, as it most likely is cracked and/or spongy. This color is a clear warning that what you are doing is not working well for you on the body, mind, and spirit levels. It takes time to remove gray energy from the aura and requires a course of treatment that can last months. The recovery period includes removing oneself from stressful situations and engaging in a combination of rest, relaxation, energy work, and time spent in nature, preferably by the ocean. The person must also seek help to find what is causing their malaise in order to recover and repair from this situation. Disease found in the body is affected by dis-ease in thoughts and emotions. The gray color in the aura reflects that something is out of balance in the person's life, which is causing them great dis-ease and discomfort.

When dark gray is seen in the aura, it represents energy manifested from working with dark forces. It also indicates a secretive person who is removing him- or herself from the positive forces of the Universe. An aura covered in dark gray will typically have black areas around it, which grow larger in time if the person continues to think, act, and engage with darker forces, while moving away from positive thinking and white light.

RECOMMENDATIONS TO REPAIR GRAY

Foods: Anything from the orange category will do well to help restore vitality and joy.

Home Décor: Go for bold, cheerful, lively colors of any bright hue. Avoid black and white.

Clothing: Same as home décor—bold and lively.

Gemstones: Hematite to remove negative energy.

Flowers: Any flowers in bright bold colors to lift the spirit and energy of the person are beneficial.

Music: Empowering, uplifting music.

Activities: Dancing and any physical activity that takes the person out of their thoughts and into breathing fresh air and moving the body.

Mantra: *I return to joy. Joy is within me, working through me now, and coursing through my veins. I have a zest for life and see all the good that is to come.*

Brown

Brown is perhaps the most misunderstood color in the aura. When people see brown, they automatically think that the color is muddy and represents a problem. This is not always the case. I have seen monks with brown in their aura, and people who work in nature resonate with a brown energy. These are typically well-grounded people who enjoy working with their hands and with tasks of this type. These monks would be the ones who would volunteer to care for the garden. Forest rangers and wood carvers often carry a brown energy. I would muse that, back in the day, many druids carried brown energy in their aura as well.

When the brown color is warm and light, it can present a light coffee color or caramel tone. This can appear in the fields of people who are in touch with the elements and have connected in a strong way with the element of earth. The color serves to ground them and will be seen in the solar plexus area, mixing with yellow to help release old emotional pain back into the earth.

Rather than seeing brown as always muddy, pay close attention to the hue of the color and where the brown color is appearing in the auric field. The presence of muddiness will better explain whether the flow is stagnant or the person has simply been working with the earth in order to ground and reconnect at the root level.

When the brown seen is truly a muddy dark brown, rather than what I would describe as a warm brown, then it is cause for concern, as the person is in a dark emotional state and is on the verge of the brown mutating into black in the aura.

RECOMMENDATIONS TO CONNECT WITH AND ENHANCE BROWN

Foods: Chocolate, carob, coffee, tea, peanuts, brown rice, and granola.

Home Décor: Brown is a very grounding color. Rather than using it as a paint color on the wall, go for hardwood floors and furniture and use khaki and caramel as accent colors on the walls.

Clothing: Brown is very grounding. It's a good color to wear when one desires to connect with their roots and feel grounded.

Gemstones: Jasper, tiger's eye, petrified wood, agate, ammonite, and feldspar.

Flowers: An herb or vegetable garden will help with brown, allowing the person to dig into the earth and plant something to nourish.

Music: Native American flute music.

Activities: Planting trees and spending time alone in nature.

Mantra: *I am connected to my roots and my ancestors. I honor those who walked the path before me and I tread lightly upon this planet with great care. I spread my branches to be of service and what I take, I replenish. I walk with the Great Spirit and the members of the animal and plant kingdoms are my brothers and sisters.*

Black

Black is the color in the aura that requires the most discernment to understand. It is very subjective and has to be read in conjunction with the other colors surrounding it. Masters of the metaphysical arts understand that black is a powerful and protective color, and they will use black to shield themselves from unwanted energy and other malevolent advances. Seeing a black shield around the aura can indicate this kind of force field being projected. This type of black shield is only projected in the most extreme and rare cases. In the overwhelming majority of situations, the auric field projected as a force field is white in color. If black remains a constant color in the aura—not just used as a temporary shield from unwanted energy advances—it indicates a person who has detached from the positive and light forces of life and the Universe.

When black appears in the aura as a ring around the field, it can indicate that there were periods of abuse in some form and that the ring was created to help shield the person from the abuse. If the ring is still large, there is usually some damage to the auric field, as the consciousness of the person attempted to pull away and out of the auric fields and escape to a higher plane after a prolonged period of abuse.

Black specks in the aura and other shapes that I have seen in black indicate physical disease and can point to health problems. I have seen black symbols, shapes, and pockets around certain organs, indicating that the energy is not flowing in this area and disease is forming.

RECOMMENDATIONS TO CONNECT WITH AND BALANCE BLACK

Foods: Not applicable.

Home Décor: Black as an accent brings power to a room. Using black wrought iron creates a protective field in the home.

Clothing: Black is worn as a protective shield and can be used to hold the energy in the auric fields. If you find yourself wearing all black too often, with no additional colors as accents, it is wise to take a moment and see if you are feeling the need for protection.

Gemstones: Black obsidian, hematite, and smoky quartz.

Flowers: White flowers actually work to connect with black energy.

Music: Not applicable.

Activities: Releasing black rings created from painful experiences requires the assistance of skilled professionals. Seek an appointment with a therapist and an energy worker to begin the healing process.

Mantra: A mantra to remove black rings would be better created after connecting with skilled professionals who will help create a plan of action to release negative energies and heal from past abuse.

Five

How the Aura Develops from Childhood into Adulthood

You can never really live anyone else's life,
not even your child's. The influence you exert
is through your own life, and what you've
become yourself.

—Eleanor Roosevelt

ccording to the ancient wisdom teachings, we form essentially a new body every seven years, all the way down to the cellular level. At the beginning of each of the seven-year cycles, we have replaced almost every cell in our body and have the opportunity to begin new and fresh. When we comprehend the renewal going on inside our bodies, the possibility exists that we can rebuild ourselves from the inside out, with our words, thoughts, actions, and deeds, restoring our physical vitality and enhancing our auric field and energy bodies. The teachings further state that at the age of 49, we have completed a full cycle of seven times seven; during this cycle, our auric and energy bodies are all open and fully complete in their manifestations.

At the age of 49, we make the choice with our higher self whether or not to evolve further into Wise Women and Wise Men, entering the sage cycle. This cycle allows us to connect even more deeply into our spiritual being and become a force of great energy to be shared with others in whatever capacity we are drawn to. At this point, we have everything we need to co-create anything we desire. We can choose to be great leaders, visionaries, and inspirational beings making a powerful impact on the world.

How the Aura Develops

The auric fields work according to the hermetic axiom of "As Above, So Below." As a soul in the higher spiritual planes prepares to enter a physical body, the information stored in that soul is transferred through the network of the seven auric layers. The information stored in this network works to create the physical body, which includes information recorded from past lives. This includes karma, memory imprints, and other information as to what type of life and lifestyle the soul is looking to create in this new lifetime. This information is then used to form and create the physical body, down to the details of genetic characteristics including hair color, skin type, and genetic defects and weaknesses as well as strengths. It's a complicated chain of events that gets even more complex with each lifetime, as memories and desires are layered from all the previous lives.

With each thought and action we take on the earthly plane, this information is recorded and stored in our aura, in the layer referred to as the auric template. Before we return for another lifetime, we meet with our guides in the higher planes and look over our akashic records. During the review of these records, we see each past life and review the areas of the world in which we lived, the families we interacted with, and the resulting karmic ties that bind us together again in a new life-time. We also decide where and how we should live and how we should look in the physical sense in order to best complete and engage in our karmic destiny and lessons to be learned. Whatever shape and style your body currently reflects in this lifetime, *love it*, for it was created especially for you, by you, in order to do the work that needs to be done in this lifetime.

The Aura Cycle from Pregnancy and Birth through Age 7

The aura changes dramatically from birth to age 7, as the physical body develops at its greatest rate. With this in mind, imagine how helpful it would be to see the aura around a crying infant and be able to under-stand what is causing its discomfort. For a condition like colic, you could see the unease and energy disruption as the pain was being felt in the etheric aura.

During pregnancy, the imprint of energy from the soul of the baby begins its descent from the higher planes down through the lower planes and helps form the seven energy layers around the infant's physical body. Once connected into the seven layers of the aura, the soul and life-force energy enter into the physical body, connecting with each of the chakras. This connection begins during the second trimester of pregnancy and grows stronger and more complete during the third trimester. In these two trimesters, specific characteristics of the child begin to form, which are being informed by the genetic imprint from the physicality of the parents and from the soul's karmic imprint. If you've ever wondered why you don't look exactly like other members of your family, your soul blueprint may have dictated that you had to have different characteristics in order to experience what you needed to in this lifetime.

By the time the baby is ready to be born, all systems are in place around the energy bodies and they are ready and waiting for the "on" button to be engaged. This occurs instantly at the moment of the first breath taken by the baby after it has left the mother's womb. In that first breath, the auric bodies and chakras are activated and begin to whirl in a pattern that is distinctive and unique for each person.

At birth, the etheric field is the most engaged auric field, interacting with the child to provide nourishment, comfort, and energy for the child to develop and grow. From birth to age 7, the openings between the spiritual planes and the physical planes are wide around each child. The body, mind, and spirit of the child are actively downloading information from the Other Side, which sets the tone and direction for this lifetime. Beyond the aura, this metaphysical opening can be seen where the soft spot of the skull remains open on children. This area does not fully close until after the age of 7. The higher conscious energy is open to the Other Side and receives a continuous flow of energy to nourish the soul as it anchors into the physical body. The energy expression of our souls is vast and it takes these seven years to adjust to drawing this powerful energy down from the expansive planes and compressing it into one physical body in order to interact on the earthly plane. This is why sleep is so important for infants and children. They are receiving an abundance of information downloaded into their auric fields. As they sleep, the auric fields process and sort the information and energy while allowing the body and mind to relax and rejuvenate.

The energy of each soul is very beautiful and pure, and this is why pregnant women glow—they are intimately connected with the higher planes during their pregnancy and are receiving love and light from the Other Side in order to form the new being inside. It truly is a miraculous event for all involved. Babies and small children spend a lot of their time, up to age 7, engaging with the other planes and developing their energy bodies.

The etheric and other energy fields are still being developed in childhood and they have not quite built up their wall of protection, which works as a buffer to slow down the intensity of how emotions and energy feel when expressed by another person, especially when expressed negatively. This is why children are startled so easily and become upset when people are arguing around them. It is very important that they live in peaceful surroundings as much as possible during these early years.

One of the reasons babies cry so often is to release pent-up energy. While their bodies are working to fill up on energy, they are also absorbing energy from the people around them because their fields are wide open. Since their auric bodies are still being formed, babies don't yet have the ability to release energy in a physical, mental, or emotional manner. They need to distribute and release some of the energy they are receiving and picking up from others around them. The act of crying allows an infant to release this energy, as well as to bring in fresh healthy oxygen to assist in their development. Babies need to cry, so keep an open mind about it when you hear them cry and know they are doing what they need to do for their development. (Unless of course they are hungry or wet; in that case, they're trying to get your attention!) Being held with a warm touch while they are releasing this energy is very helpful at this time, as it is for any adult.

The importance and power of touch is often underestimated in regard to child development. Studies have shown that babies in hospitals and orphanages who were held often in a loving manner fared much better than babies in the same care who only had their needs tended to—meaning that they were fed and changed, but they received no further affection. The children who were not touched as much did not grow as well and were more sickly. The power of touch can be very healing and is felt in all of the auric fields as well as in the physical body.

All of the seven layers are forming around the body of a child, and by the age of 7, the etheric body has pretty much formed into the shape and strength it will hold for the present lifetime. The soul is also fully engaged in the physical body, residing in the heart chakra area. The etheric layer soon begins its work to support the body, gathering energy from light and sleep. This energy is then drawn into the physical body and enters each of the chakras and the organs. The etheric body continues this work on a daily basis to deliver the best energy it can to the physical body. How much energy it is able to deliver, though, is based on the quality of the energy it can receive from the auric bodies. If the aura becomes sluggish and cloudy—whether due to poor nutrition, lack of sleep, stress, smoking in the home, drugs, alcohol abuse, auric damage, or shock—then it is not able to pull in and store the energy it needs to deliver to the body, organs, and chakras.

The Aura Cycle from Age 7 through 14

From age 7 to age 14, the auric body that develops the most is the mental body. This is why education at the elementary level is so important, as the mental field is soaking up all the information it can during this seven-year period. This is the best time to learn anything, from foreign languages to math to science. It also explains why children walk around asking their parents hundreds of questions each day that begin with the word *why*. Their mental field is pushing them to understand and interpret everything around them. What they learn at this stage sets the foundation for everything they will do in adulthood.

What is introduced to a child at this age will stay with them throughout their lifetime in their mental field. Their minds are wide open and spongelike; they soak up all the information provided to them. Their creativity is easily stimulated and they will explore any outlet offered to them. When I work with my clients who are looking to increase their business intuition, I begin by taking them back to their childhood and asking them what they most loved to do between the ages of 7 and 14. In most cases, what you loved to do during this time and what you thought you might like to be and do when you "grew up" gives clear signals as to what your mental field enjoyed and was attracted to doing back when it was not bound by societal constraints and pressures. Think back to this time in your life to find clues as to whether you are following what your mental field most enjoyed doing, as this will provide guidance in your career aspirations.

As a parent, a teacher, or someone who works with children at this age, it is important to understand that their mental field is developing rapidly and that the child is seeking all the knowledge and information they can grab. What they experience and learn during this seven-year cycle will serve to inspire them for the rest of their lives. What they experience can cause a direct effect on how they feel about themselves, the world, and others as they learn from direct experience and observation of their parents, teachers, and other adults in their lives. There are many computer programs and games introduced to children at this age, which is just a part of the world we live in. Computers have their place, but it is also important for parents to engage in mentally challenging activities during this time of the child's development. From age 7 to 14, children love puzzles, maps, and games that allow them to think and plan. Checkers, chess, board games, map reading to find directions to a destination, and planning and planting a garden are all activities that will stimulate the mental field. In addition, when children are engaged in sports at this age, they learn the values of teamwork, practice, and strategizing.

The Aura Cycle from Age 14 through 21

Seeing the auric field in teenagers can be extremely beneficial, as often they are not open to discussing their problems. The auric fields can show whether they are depressed, emotionally overwhelmed, potentially abusing drugs or alcohol, or just engaged in the typical emotional ups and downs and hormonal imbalances of the teenage years.

From age 14 to 21, the auric body that develops the most is the emotional body. The emotional field is connected to the second (sacral) chakra and the onset of puberty coincides with the emotional development. It is during this seven-year cycle that the tone for relationships is created in the field of the person. From the relationships with parents, siblings, relatives, friends, and love interests, the emotional body is forming intricate patterns that will relate to how it will react to these relationships in the future.

It is not just the experiences received during this time that determine how the person will connect with others in relationship settings; there are also the matters of karmic destiny and past lifetimes that will affect the person. Some of this destiny was set into place with the chosen astrological sign.

It is important to note that just as it is extremely helpful to understand the importance of education when children are in the mental state from 7 to 14, it is just as important to have patience and understanding with young adults as they are forming their emotional body. During the period of 14 to 21, they are also learning how to connect with other people as potential relationship partners.

The emotional state is the most chaotic when forming and—combined with the hormone development of puberty—the systems of young adults are overwhelmed and their emotional outbursts are par for the course. At times, they need to have emotional outlets and outbursts, similar to when the infant cries, as the energy buildup has become so strong that it needs to be released. Understanding this and helping to direct them to positive outlets and methods of communication can help during this seven-year period, as well as understanding that what the young adult says during this time is often affected by the overflow of emotions and shouldn't be taken personally. This is why young adults are prone to fights with friends and then are able to make up again within days or even hours. When the overflow of emotion is released, the fields calm down and the mental body is able to resume activity.

We have all been through this process, but it can be easy to forget as an adult, since we are no longer completely overwhelmed by the emotional overload received during this cycle. Each person handles this change differently according to the changes in their physical body and their emotional field. The mental field holds the information from what it has recorded for the previous seven years while observing relationships. If the young girl has seen a confident and secure mother who has worked to impress self-esteem in the young girl, she will carry this information into her tumultuous teen years. If the young girl has seen her father be respectful, loving, and attentive to the mother in a mature manner, she will seek out relationships that offer her the same attention. If a young boy has seen a warm, loving, and secure mother, he will seek out the same as a partner in the future; the patterns he has viewed as to how the father treated the mother will affect him as well. The child is always viewing the actions of the parent, both as a role model and in observation of how they should feel about themselves.

For example, if the mother does not feel attractive and is obsessed with her physical looks, the daughter will observe this and the potential is high that she will have self-doubt over her looks and self-worth. If the mother feels that her physical attractiveness is her only asset, or the father places tremendous value on work and material assets, this will be picked up by the children to be emulated or sought after in their relationship partners. What the children have seen and experienced during this seven-year cycle will play into their emotional fields as they mature into adulthood.

The Aura Cycle from Age 21 through 49

From age 21 to age 49, the astral body, etheric template body, celestial body, and ketheric body are fully engaged and ready to develop further with conscious effort. These fields are referred to as the spiritual bodies, and they respond quickly to focused thought and intentions. They are more fluid and lighter and thus respond to energetic vibrations easily. Music, for example, affects these fields and engages them, as do light and color. Higher conscious thoughts and spiritual works such as prayer and meditation also have an immediate effect upon these layers. The aura is stimulated, grows, and declines as described throughout this book depending on what it experiences in the physical, mental, emotional, and spiritual fields on a daily basis.

The Aura Cycle from age 49 Onward

At the culmination of the seventh cycle (7 years x 7 cycles = 49), the auric field has matured into its full state. The aura is fully capable and ready to assist the person to pursue any spiritual journeys they desire. As the physical body slows down, the sexual drive lowers as women enter menopause and testosterone levels decrease for men. The physical body is able to continue to have sex for pleasure, but the drive for procreation is no longer present. The emotional and mental fields have matured during these cycles and, in most cases, the emotional field finds a sense of contentment and understanding. The mental field has collected a vast library of information and knowledge and is entering the period of becoming a wise sage. When conscious of this progress at all levels, a person can channel the energy from these fields and connect them into the spiritual fields in order to delve deeper into the spiritual essence of their being.

How to See and Enhance the Aura

When seeing the aura, we are seeing the universal life force called *chi*, or universal energy. This energy moves in a spiral pattern, similar to the appearance of a DNA molecule. Universal energy spirals from the sun, the moon, the planets, and the stars down to Earth. It also spirals down from the higher spiritual planes through each soul into the auric fields and into the physical body.

As well as universal chi, we each have our own personal chi that begins at birth when we take our first breath. With each breath we inhale, we are drawing in the chi floating around us; with each exhale, we are releasing chi from within us back out into our energy fields. Chi is pure energy that is neither positive nor negative; it just is, and therefore it can be charged with positive or negative sources. With each breath we take, we can visualize pulling in clear and pure air into our auric fields and positive energy into the physical body. With each exhale of breath, we can visualize removing negative energy from our auric fields and releasing stagnant energy from the physical body.

A helpful practice to raise and clear the energy in the auric body can be done daily in two easy steps and will only take about five minutes each day.

Exercise: Raising the Energy in the Aura

Step One: Take three deep breaths. With each breath in, visualize pulling clear pure air and positive energy into the body. Hold the breath for a count of three seconds while continuing to visualize the pure energy circulating inside you. Then exhale outward forcefully through the mouth. As you exhale, visualize all negative energy leaving your body and see it floating away into the air, moving away from you, and dissipating into nothingness.

Step Two: Visualize the white light of the aura around your body. See yourself covered in a dome of bright light—a warm, vibrant white light that forms an oval shape around your entire body. Know that this light is the essence of life and contains the pure divine rays of universal energy. This light forms a shield that protects your body and provides life-enhancing energy to you every day. While visualizing the white light around your aura, speak this affirmation out loud:

May the pure loving light of the Universe surround me and fill me with pure energy, pure love, and white light. I ask to receive only that which is for my highest and best good. My auric bodies are filled with white light energy and are functioning at their highest capacity. I give thanks.

The combination of speaking this affirmation aloud along with visualizing the white light in the aura helps to focus your conscious mind to become aware of the aura and its protective field. It also begins to establish a practice of drawing energy into the fields and releasing stagnant energy, which is the first step to learning how to expand the auric field as a shield.

Exercise: How to See the Aura Using the Physical Eyes

Step One: Find a person who is willing to work with you and will allow you to stare at them to see their aura. Have them sit sideways on a stool in front of a plain white wall so that you are looking at their profile. (A stool is preferred, if possible, because you want to clearly see the back of their head without the back of a chair interfering.)

Step Two: Look at the back of their head and then at the wall behind their head. Now let your eyes relax. Do not focus looking directly at their head; instead gaze next to their head where its edge meets with the wall. Relax your eyes and gaze at this area. Within a minute or two, you will see the first level of the aura, which will appear as a white border around the physical body.

Step Three: Once you see their aura, ask them to think about something that makes them really happy. As they connect with this emotion, you will see their aura extend outward. You will be able to observe when they stop thinking of the happy thought, as the aura will shrink back down in size.

At first, you may only see a light color or a muted color—do not worry! The more you practice, the more your skill will develop and you will begin to see the colors around the person's body.

Exercise: How to See the Aura Using Your Field of Consciousness (and Eventually Using the Third Eye)

Many people who practice seeing an aura are able to see the first layer and the white glow around the body but find it more difficult to see the colors around the person. For some, it is too disconcerting to continue to stare at the person for a length of time, since both parties become uncomfortable. The person who is unable to see the colors of the aura will grow frustrated, which will ruin any chance of seeing the aura. The person who is willing to be stared at will become bored and physically uncomfortable sitting still for a long length of time, and they will move and shift their position. For a beginning aura reader, each time the person moves, it throws off their center point (where they began to stare at the white border), and so they have to reset their gaze and begin anew. If this is a problem when trying to see colors for the first time, an alternate choice would be to ask the person if you can observe them while they are sleeping, as they will be lying still and you can sit for a while and gaze at their field. You can also practice seeing the aura through your field of consciousness, which can be an easier way to see the aura without distraction. In addition, with practice, seeing auras in this capacity allows you to see the other auric fields, which are more difficult to view with the physical eyes.

A powerful and protective way to connect with the auric field through your consciousness is by first energizing the white light around your aura. This focuses your energy and raises the vibrations within the body and energy fields. This stimulation excites the higher self and calls it forth to send greater energy to the body.

Step One: Sit comfortably in a position where your arms and legs are unencumbered and your posture is such that you can breathe deeply and easily without obstruction. Close your eyes and take a deep breath inward to the count of three. Hold the breath for the count of three and then release it to the count of three. Each time you inhale, visualize beautiful clear air coming into you. Exhale each breath fully from the mouth, blowing out any negative energy. Repeat this process three times.

Now visualize the pure white light of universal energy. While doing this, raise and hold both of your arms into the air (forming a large *V*). Visualize the white light drawing closer to you and speak out loud three times:

I am surrounded by the pure white light.
Nothing but good can come to me,
nothing but good can come from me.
I give thanks.

While speaking this out loud, continue to hold your arms open in this *V* and feel the chi falling through your auric fields, into your arms, and down into your body. Hold this position for another moment until you feel the energy and know that it is surrounding you in your field. Then draw your arms back down, bending them at the elbow and crossing them across your chest, making an *X* over your chest with your arms. This seals the white light into the body and the auric field. Once this is sealed, you may bring your arms to rest at your sides, keeping your palms open and relaxed.

Step Two: Clear your mind and focus on the energy flowing around you. Once you can detect the energy field around you, see if you can determine how far out this field goes around your body. There are many ways in which to do this, and you will have to practice to see which way works for you intuitively. One exercise is to hold your hands over your body until you connect with and sense the energy field. Once you connect with it, allow the energy to draw your hands outward until you have reached the end of that field.

Step Three: Bring your hands back down to rest, keeping the palms open and relaxed. It's now time to focus your attention on a plant or tree in front of you as you attempt to expand your consciousness to connect with the tree. Visualize the tree in your mind and ask to connect with the energy of the tree. Continue to breathe slowly and deeply in and out during the entire process. Now visualize your energy field and see it reach out and expand until it connects with the energy field of the tree.

As you practice this exercise, it is likely that you will first connect with the tree using your field of consciousness rather than directly through the third eye. Through your consciousness field, you can connect with the energy of any living organism. This is how it should occur, as the third eye should never be forced to open.

When you are finished connecting with the tree or plant, pull your conscious energy back into your field and visualize closing and sealing the field around you. Breathe deeply in and out and form the white light shield back around you. Seal the shield by crossing your arms again over your chest to form an *X*. It is always helpful to ground the body after doing this energy work. A piece of chocolate works quickly to ground the bodies back into the physical field after energy work—and it tastes great!

As you continue this exercise each day along with your spiritual practices, you will naturally raise the energy in your body by cleansing and clearing all of your auric fields and chakras. By doing this, the energy will elevate over time and the third eye will open when the energy is purified and engaged and ready to open naturally, which is the best course. It is wise to allow the body and mind to follow the guidance of the higher self in these matters and not force any of the energy fields or the third eye to open before they are ready.

When the time and energy feel right and you know that you are ready to look through the third eye, bring your conscious mind into focus and connect with the energy slightly above your eyes in the forehead area. Visualize energy around this area and see the area opening like a portal. As this portal opens, you will feel a tingling sensation, and part of your consciousness will venture out from this area. At this point, it is important to maintain focus and guide your energy toward the tree that you wish to connect with.

When you are first working with energy at this level, it is safer to connect with energy in nature, such as a tree, rather than with a person. You are opening up an area that is vulnerable until you have created a very strong auric field of protection. The best course is to first build up psychic self-defense practices. It is also important to have a good working knowledge of and practice how to protect and shield your auric energy field before opening the third eye.

Raising Consciousness Connection with Your Children through Divine Feminine Energy

There is great power and responsibility granted to women in order to bring life into the world. While pregnancy and giving birth are life-altering and affirming experiences, they do not a mother make in full. There are many mothers in the world who are loved deeply by people to whom they did not give birth. These women truly understand the power and connection to the Divine Feminine. They know that the spirit of the Great Mother lives in every woman. To be a mother is to embody the attributes of love, comfort, and generosity while caring for and honoring oneself. These acts evoke the Divine Feminine energy, allowing it to pour forth, nourishing all who enter her space. When a woman lives in this energy, she lightens the load of the world, brings peace to her family, inspires her friends, and rocks a man to his core.

When a man connects to the feminine energy inside of him, he moves into balance and gains a deeper understanding of the cycle of life and the connection to all living beings. When he lives in balance with this energy, he brings a solid strength to his family. He is connected to the life force and becomes a shining knight in service to the Great Mother and connects to his shaman side.

Inside every woman and man, the Great Mother stirs and requests that her presence be known and validated. Some energy work can be accomplished through meditation, visualization, and affirmation, but when working directly with the Great Mother, she insists upon action.

Here is what she asks that you do in order to connect with the Divine Feminine energy of the Great Mother:

- When you look upon someone with kind eyes and a smile, you honor the Great Mother.

- When you care for another who is ill or lonely, you are the touch of the Great Mother.

- When you stand to protect another soul and speak out against injustice, you are the voice of the Great Mother.

- When you love unconditionally—children, nature, animals, and yourself—you embody the Great Mother.

- When your life is rich with the greatest joys you could imagine and you see a child who is hurting and you would trade everything in order to bring them comfort, you are the Great Mother.

Six

THE LINGERING EFFECT OF THOUGHT ON THE AURIC BODY

The most healing act one can ever do for another person is to send them love. The most healing act one can do to heal one's self is to love yourself. Love is the greatest power that exists. Yet in order to love our self, we most know our self and, in that knowing, find peace. To find peace, we must first ask the question, "What is peace?"

—Kala Ambrose

In our unconscious state of being as humans, we often fail to realize and appreciate what we have in front of us and are unable to see how much we would miss it until it is taken away from us. You don't know what you've got until it's gone. Likewise, we often don't stop to see if we are at peace with the world and ourselves; we only become aware of peace when it's absent. The question we must ask ourselves is, "Do we squander time when we could be at peace, choosing instead to indulge in misery and complaints, until something truly awful happens to make us realize that our lives were pretty peaceful?"

Many cultures try to teach that peace is a state of mind. It's taught in the Catholic Mass when each person turns in a full circle, greets each person they see, holds their hand, looks them in the eye, and says, "Peace be with you." Buddhist monks teach meditation, expressing the concept that to meditate is to be unaffected and calm while chaos occurs around you—to remain at peace while others panic.

In reviewing the concept of peace in its most simplistic definition, it is described as the absence of war. Could this refer to the war within each of us, as we struggle against ourselves? Is it possible to know peace without first knowing war? Must we experience friction in order to know its release?

In the laws of physics, friction occurs when two objects come into contact with each other. The amount of friction can be measured in terms of how much force is required before motion of some type occurs. We see this when two sticks are rubbed together until a spark is created, resulting in fire. When you take a step, you create friction to push your foot off the ground to take the next step. When waves break on the shore, friction is created. It is the same with people and the energies of their auras: a kiss creates friction, two ideas or ideologies clashing create friction, and a lively conversation creates friction.

While pondering these scenarios, the question arises, "What if we need places and people to help us find peace by creating chaos around us?" Let us consider friction in a new light. We often think of friction in a negative light. But what if, by grand design, we inadvertently create friction as part of a master plan? Could the laws of physics and friction be the entire catalyst for our journey on the earthly plane? After all, does not the friction of a grain of sand in the oyster create the pearl?

What if every action does have a reaction, and we hold the key to peace? What if the answer lies in the fact that we haven't understood at what price peace comes, or that peace has a price at all? Perhaps we have a larger role to play in consciously creating the state of peace than we think.

Perhaps each person who enters our lives, whether for a brief moment or a lifetime relationship, does so when they need that experience and, in that meeting, we experience friction in order to understand inner peace. As we continue to cry aloud en masse to "give peace a chance," have we been looking outward for so long that we've lost sight of all that we know to be true? Maybe the answers we seek and the help we long for can actually be found within ourselves.

If we are, as the ancient teachings say, "all one," **then we have the capability to come to peace with every thought, word, action, and deed that we do and that others do unto us.** The challenge is then presented to come to peace with every experience you have had in this lifetime, including all of the experiences orchestrated by you and when you experienced something through the design of another. If you can find peace in all thoughts, words, actions, and deeds, and in each experience that presents itself to you, then you have the power to heal yourself from the inside out on all levels. It is when we don't live in peace that we carry tumultuous and chaotic energy in our emotional and mental fields. The longer this energy remains in our fields, the more thought we give to it. The more thought we give to something negative and unhealthy, the greater it grows. Simple thoughts, when given enough energy, can grow into powerful forms of energy in the aura; these are described as thought forms.

In this chapter, you'll learn how your thoughts affect you and your auric fields and how to clear your energy of thought forms.

Thought Forms Created in the Auric Fields

When we have a thought that upsets us deeply on an emotional level for a long period of time, or if we obsess about it often, we give it a tremendous amount of energy. We have the power to give positive energy to a thought, which then helps manifest that positive thought into something good in our life, but many people have not yet learned to focus their long-term thoughts on positive outcomes and manifestations. It's backward, but the majority of the time, we focus more on the thoughts that upset us the most.

When we focus on a thought long enough, it begins to take shape in the auric fields. The shape looks like a little gray cloud. We are "creators" and, in essence, we are creating our own weather pattern around us in our auric field. We can be full of anger (volcanic eruptions), have a waver of depression (low-pressure system), or feel warm and sunny (like the tropics). Since we create with every thought, a negative thought that we focus on every day gives part of our energy to that thought, and it begins to create a small gray form. Once the thought has created a form, it is able to hold energy more efficiently. We are, in effect, telling our system that this thought is very important and that's why we are giving it so much energy every day. The auric field responds to our commands. What we give thought and attention to is what we are telling the fields to manifest! Did you know that you had this much power?

If we continue to think about an emotionally upsetting or negative thought, it will eventually move from the gray cloud shape and form into a stronger mass that can hold even more energy. The mass will turn itself into a shape that resembles the type of thought it receives on a continued basis. These shapes can be seen in the auric fields and are referred to as *thought forms*. Thought forms, given enough energy, can grow to become strong energetic creations and cause blocks in the way of what you want to achieve in life.

The law of attraction is based upon the understanding that energy follows thought, and focused thought manifests outwardly. Many people's thoughts and emotions generate from the first three chakras: the survival center of the root chakra, the desire of the sacral chakra, and the seat of will in the solar plexus. On a daily basis, the thoughts originating from the emotional and mental bodies are short-lived, though the field records each thought. As we go about our day saying things like, "Ooo, I like this" or "I hate that," each thought is recorded and stored in the mental and emotional fields. These fields are programmed to remember the emotion and thought surrounded by each statement. The next time you encounter a similar experience, place, or thing, the auric fields react. They begin to vibrate and recognize the stimuli and respond accordingly—"Ooo, we like this," or "We hate that." The thought forms begin to release the corresponding energy into the auric fields and the physical body.

Each thought we express outwardly to another person affects their auric fields. When we say something cruel to someone, they are hit by the intensity of the energy directed at them and it is stored in their emotional and mental auric fields. When we say something wonderful, they also receive this energy. Unfortunately, in our current period of evolution, we tend to express negative thoughts with a stronger energy outburst than we do when expressing something positive. The result is that the negative experiences carry ten times more weight and hit the person very hard in all of their auric fields.

Thankfully, a safety system was built into our fields in order to save us from ourselves. Most of us do not hold on to a thought for days at a time; our thoughts are scattered and move quickly from place to place. Many people only on the power of thought to manifest things they desire, and they will suggest that you focus on these thoughts all the time. While it is indeed a beautiful gift, it is also very powerful. As a teacher of the ancient wisdom teachings, it is my duty to my students and to all who read this book to convey the full magnitude of this power. To teach about only half of the story would be remiss. It is also important to have the knowledge of how thoughts affect others and how they can affect your karmic destiny. For example, if you only learned to focus your thoughts on getting money, without any consideration as to what your thoughts did to others or how the world was being affected by these thoughts, how do you think this would play out when reviewed in your akashic records on the Other Side in your life review?

It is very important to understand the power of thought and how our emotions can overtake our thoughts and cause us to do things we would not normally do. The auric fields are a safety net to help us sort through our thoughts and emotions. If you want to manifest something, it takes time and repetition to build the thought form in order to manifest it into being. The time that it takes to build this form gives you and your spirit guides the opportunity to consider what you are thinking about manifesting, in order to create something that is good for you on the physical, mental, emotional, and spiritual levels.

Exercise: Be the Master Creator of Your Thoughts for a Day

If you find that you are impatient and wish that your thoughts would manifest into what you think about on a daily basis, I invite you to take one day and write down every thought and emotion you have. If each of those thoughts and emotions were able to instantly manifest into your life, what effect would you have created for yourself and the world around you?

As an example, imagine a person cut you off in traffic this morning on your way to work. What would you think about and wish for them when this occurred? Perhaps that person was a father of four having a bad morning; if he had been instantly and literally affected by your thoughts directed at him, would he be going home to his children at the end of the day?

What about you and your life? How did you feel when you looked in the mirror this morning? Did you give your body beautiful, life-affirming thoughts so that it can glow in health and well-being? Where did your thoughts wander off to today? If every thought would instantly manifest into being, what would you have created in your home, in your body, with your friends and loved ones, and at work?

When first doing this exercise, it's easy to run with it and think of all the fun things you would wish for and create. Try to think about a day when you are very busy and stressed and your thoughts run away with you—what do you create on those days? The exercise is meant to remind you that at this juncture of our evolution, we don't create instantly, and that is for good reason. Even more importantly, we don't give enough thought to what we do think about from moment to moment, including what our thoughts are creating in our auric fields.

Shapes and Symbols in the Auric Fields

Thought forms can be stored in the auric fields, and energy held in the fields for a long period of time eventually creates a body or field for itself, which manifests into a shape or symbol. These shapes and symbols can be positive or negative, depending upon what energy they have been created with and what energy they continue to receive as they grow in form and strength.

Here are some of the most common shapes and symbols that I have seen in auras over the years:

Animal totems: People who work with their psychic and spiritual abilities can learn how to connect with an animal totem. This is an animal spirit that they connect with and imbibe the spirit and characteristics of. Shamans have strong animal totems, as do people who work in the magical and spiritual realms. As they learn how to connect with their animal totems, these people bring this energy into their auric fields. Those who master working with the auric fields at this level have also learned how to astral project their image and may choose to project their animal totem in the astral realms rather than their physical appearance. In the Harry Potter books and movies, this was called a patronus, and the students learned to project their patronus as a protective energy shield.

Black ring: A black ring around the aura generally indicates abuse that the person has received during this lifetime, which has affected the auric field and requires repair.

Black shield: This should not be confused with a black aura. A black aura indicates the person is withdrawing from life and turning away from light and vitality; a black shield is a force field created by a person who has mastery of the auric fields and understands how to create this shield for brief periods of time as a protective measure.

Black spots: It is important to pay attention to which particular field (mental, emotional, etc.) the spots are in; this will indicate unbalance and negative energy that is manifesting in this field. If left untreated, black spots will grow, cause discomfort, and become problematic.

Cracks: As discussed in previous chapters, when the aura hardens, it begins to crack and these cracks can be seen in the aura. They resemble skin that has dried and cracked or has cuts or scratches.

Jagged lines: These lines typically indicate that the person has been abusing drugs or alcohol and it is disrupting the flow of the auric fields. If this continues for a long period of time, it reshapes the aura and thickens the fields, which create blockages. This causes the energy to work much harder to get through each field and move into the body. This is actually the effect the person is trying to achieve, by using the intoxicants to detach themselves from feeling and thinking, but the long-term effects can be devastating.

Jagged lines indicate blockages in the auric field.

Lightning bolts: I typically see these with explosive bursts of red when a person is very angry. It always amazes me and makes me think that, in each auric field, we have a tiny manifestation of the Greek god Zeus, who threw thunderbolts when he went to war. It also makes me glad that we are not yet powerful enough to create and manifest every thought we have. What chaos would ensue if we could toss this energy at each other any stronger or more forcefully than we already do?!

Orbs: White orbs can appear in the aura, often in streaks because they move quickly. The orbs indicate the presence of spiritual beings in the aura; sometimes these are loved ones who have passed on and are visiting the person.

Pulsing waves: When I observe the aura of someone who is in a loving and peaceful state, their aura pulsates. It moves in and out slightly, like the waves in the ocean. The overall effect is calming and feels wonderful. Simply being in their presence radiates warmth and comfort, and others enjoy being in their company.

Sacred symbols: I've seen a tremendous variety of symbols in the aura; each is as unique as the person who resonates with them. The symbols include Celtic designs, Sanskrit symbols, magical symbols, and symbols of sacred geometry. Seeing these symbols in the auric fields is almost always positive and indicates what the person is connected to and working on in one or more of the auric fields in their life. In a sense, they are forming a crest on their auric shield, representing who they are and what energy they are aligning themselves with. This can be detected energetically by others who interact with and engage in the auric fields, such as people who work with magic and psychic abilities.

Silver sparkles: As mentioned earlier, these can indicate pregnancy if they are seen in the auric field continuously. If the silver sparkle appears and then moves on, like the twinkling of a star, it usually indicates the presence of a being from the higher planes who is visiting the person.

Spirit guides: Many spirit guides who choose to show themselves in the auric fields take on the appearance of who they were in a previous life or the occupation they are connected with in the auric field. Examples include an ancient Chinese apothecary who is now working with a Western doctor, a Native American shaman working to help a healer connect to earth medicine, or a Greek philosopher working to help a person with their conscious understanding of the Universe at large.

Spongy holes: When the aura becomes soggy, it gapes open and creates holes that give it the appearance of Swiss cheese or a sponge. The energy slows down and oozes out from the spongy material.

Seven

HEALING TECHNIQUES FOR ENHANCING THE AURIC FIELDS

In every culture and in every medical tradition before ours, healing was accomplished by moving energy.

—Albert Szent-Györgyi,
Nobel Laureate in Medicine

We are all energy beings surrounded by and enveloped in various degrees of energy and motion. As we've discussed, our chi energy is a force field encompassing our body, and the colors seen in the aura and energy bodies can be detected through careful study of the aura and the chakra colors. Disease in the body can often be detected in the aura before it manifests in the physical body. A person who studies auras can read much information from a person's aura, including their mood, emotions, and many aspects of their personality.

After you are comfortable with connecting to the auric energy field and seeing it, the next step is to learn how to expand it. This is accomplished by enhancing the auric shield, which protects the person from negative energy being directed toward them and from unintentional absorption of energy from other beings.

The auric bodies have an inherent wisdom that cares for the body and keeps it running, in spite of the challenges it receives on a daily basis, like poor diet, lack of nutrition, stress, pollution, lack of sleep, overwork, and exposure to viruses and germs. That's good news, but there is a way to enhance your body's ability to heal, restore, and evolve.

Ancient Healing Techniques from the Mystery Temples

The ancient wisdom teachings from Egypt and Greece taught how to connect with the spirit bodies in an axiom described as "As Above, So Below." In its essence, this explains the connection between the Universe (the macrocosm) and the Individual (the microcosm) and how the two are intertwined and reflect back to each other.

Earlier I wrote that you change on a cellular level every seven years, and so you have the ability to create an entirely new energy force field around you. This can be accomplished, in part, by becoming aware of your thoughts and actively changing what you believe, how you think, and what you choose to manifest in your life. By engaging in these activities, you can change the energy you bring into your auric field, which in turn changes the energy that floats down into the chakras and the physical body.

In the ancient mystery temples, healing techniques and procedures were designed with the individual in mind. The patient would meet with a team of holistic meta-physicians (healers) who worked to create a healing regime to connect with and heal on the body, mind, and spiritual levels. The consultation would begin with an interview of the patient, gathering their medical history and their life history. The group of healers would then discuss and create the best course of treatment for each patient on an individual basis.

The healing treatment began with the patient staying overnight in one of the rooms of the temple specifically designed for healing. The patient would drink an herbal tea concoction that helped them to sleep soundly. As they slept, a priestess would stay with them throughout the night, conducting light energy work over the aura and etheric body.

During the following days and weeks, the patient would receive healing in the physical body through massage, herbs, potions, and even surgery, when required. Some of the oldest surgical tools discovered originate from ancient Egypt. The patient would also speak with a healer, who would listen to what was going on in their personal life in order to relieve stress and pain and allow the patient to heal the mind and restore—an ancient version of therapy or counseling.

In conjunction, healing at the energetic level included sounds (bells, music, and bowls were played) and lights (different rooms were assigned by color and access to sunlight as needed for the patient). Healing techniques and natural elements were used, including treatments by fire (sauna-type rooms for sweating out toxins), water (bathing in waterfalls and pools with minerals added), air (breathing rituals designed to calm the nerves and bring in new energy), and earth (grounding; natural foods, flowers, fruits, and vegetables; and crystal healing techniques).

How the Connection Moved Away from Body/Mind/Spirit

We've discussed how the Industrial Revolution created in the Western world a shift from a connection with nature to a focus on mass production. During this same era, the American Civil War and then two world wars refocused the evolution of medicine toward repairing the physical body from trauma. With advancements in technology, tremendous leaps were made in medicine, including li transplants, reattaching limbs, and delicate internal surgeries. There is no doubt that the field of medicine has advanced over the last few centuries in surgical techniques and research with gene therapy.

The unfortunate side effect of this time of advancement, wars, overcrowded conditions in the cities, and rapid growth is that the head and mind detached from the heart and soul. During this time in the developed world, we lost the idea of the body/mind/spirit connection and moved toward connecting only with the mind.

Medical science (representing the figurative head) became so enamored with what could be attached, replaced, and/or removed from the physical body (such as tumors, growths, and diseased organs) that it forgot about the heart and soul of the person, which also have a direct effect on the health of the body. Medical care began to focus on patching up and eradicating disease in the physical body, rather than exploring the idea of proactive health care and avoidance of disease. This regimen places the person in a loop of illness, because the root cause of the problem, where the disease is first manifesting in the mental and emotional auric bodies, is never treated. The result is that the physical disorder is cleared from the body for a short time only to reappear later if it has not also been released from the auric fields.

There is little understanding on the part of many physicians of the body/mind/spirit connection. Examples include patients with stage four cancers who come to the physician for treatment and the physician will say that even with treatment, there is nothing much that can be done for them. In some cases, the physician is then rendered speechless when that patient later appears to them with the cancer completely gone from their body. The only term they have for this phenomenon is *spontaneous remission;* the patient and their family have no term for it other than *miracle.*

In many situations, this is how the healing occurs: The patient's family and friends shower the patient with prayer and healing thoughts, which send powerful white light energy to his or her auric fields. At the same time, the patient, realizing that death could be imminent, mentally and emotionally decides to make huge changes in their life. They let go of anger, worry, and stress. Many times they go away to naturally beautiful places, quit their jobs, and do things they have always wanted to do. They begin to live a life of ease and satisfaction. If they are successful in changing the energy in their mental and emotional fields and replacing them completely with new energy with no attachments to old memories—including guilt, regret, remorse, anger, and worry—the auric fields are cleared. At this point, the auric fields have the potential to do their best work and heal from the higher planes down through the mental and emotional planes and into the chakras, which then spin the energy through the organs, the nervous system, and all parts of the body. If the body has not become too worn down over time by the illness, and if the auric fields are able to now function at full capacity, there is a tremendous opportunity for the body to be healed and restored.

In ancient times, temples were created with this healing regime in mind and the person would spend the time there needed to recuperate, restore, and renew the body, mind, and spirit. They spent time in spa-like atmospheres with warm baths, connected to their higher selves, and were able to rest peacefully without a care in the world. There were people to speak with and one could release the burdens and pain carried inside. For some, it was simply their time to pass on and they were given loving care and treatment while their body continued its journey to shut down and prepare for the soul to be released and journey to the Other Side. In these cases, the patient was taught how to prepare for the transition of death, rather than to fear it and avoid discussing it. What happened to the person as the time of death approached was explained in detail—how the physical body would shut down and what would happen at the last breath as the cords detached and the auric field made its preparations to pull the energy back up into the higher planes. Just as a system was in place before birth and the energy cords and fields were anchored into the physical body, a similar process occurs as the physical body prepares for death; the cords prepare to untie and float back to the higher planes, carrying the soul and the essence of the person. The process of dying was taught to each person so they understood it and were at peace with it. It was not something to be feared but rather understood as the next part of the soul's journey.

As a culture, the Western world reveres celebrities who feel pressure to appear forever young. They have poisons like Botox needled into their face to show that their physical body is still holding up, in a bizarre concept of outer beauty that is being perpetuated. This is a reflection of the culture still in the third (solar plexus) chakra and still struggling with self-esteem issues and lack of connection. In the Western world, the focus is on the physical body as if it is the only part of a person that exists. By working on the physical body, the majority of medical establishments are only focusing on one-third of the healing process.

The Root of the Disconnection from Body/Mind/Spirit

When looking at this disconnection from body/mind/spirit, there is always a root cause to the problem. The medical disconnection is just one cause of the root problem.

As we look back into Western history, we travel back a few hundred years to the Dark Ages. During this time, scientists and doctors were maligned, threatened, and at times tortured for their research at the hands of religious fanatics who did not want science to conflict with their religious campaigns. Doctors were not even allowed to look at a deceased body in order to study it for anatomy purposes, and many medical practices were forbidden due to superstitious religious beliefs.

During this time in history, ancient techniques from the mystery temples were passed down in secret from generation to generation, since there was an active campaign by religious sects to destroy the scientists, shamans, Wise Women and Cunning Men, and natural healers. Some reports state that more than three million women and men were killed for heretical practices during these dark times; the majority were women who were healers and midwives. It became a crime punishable by death for women to offer any type of holistic or herbal healing or to assist women in childbirth as a midwife.

The old ways of healing were almost completely eradicated in the Western world during the Dark Ages, as healers and scientists were tortured and killed along with their families, so it is understandable why science and religion parted company. Religion at that time was in the business of working with government to overtake other cultures and force them to convert to the official religion. The old ways were destroyed in every way possible. Any pagan sacred site found in Europe soon had a church built on top of it. Any gatherings not sanctioned by the Church were made illegal, and anyone caught attending such a gathering was arrested. Any person who practiced folk remedies or used natural herbs and incantations was labeled a witch and burned or otherwise killed. In short, anyone who disagreed with the precepts of the Church was destroyed.

One of the most destructive parts of this campaign—second only to the massive loss of lives and families destroyed—is that the campaign also focused on having people turn to a priest or preacher to be the representative of God. No longer could a person have a direct connection with the universal source or a personal understanding of the spirit and divine energy that lived within them and in nature. The focus was to remove the entire concept and understanding that each person has tremendous power and potential living within and around them and that this is their natural-born gift and birthright. People were forced to believe that they were powerless and had to reach out to the almighty Church to get power. If they in any way believed something different, they were damned for eternity and would burn in a lower-level dimension called hell.

This is not easy to accomplish—changing thousands of years of ancient practices, natural connections to self and the earth, and overall beliefs throughout a large part of the world. It was accomplished over a two-hundred-year period by torturing and killing millions of people, overtaking all of their sacred sites, burning all texts and materials they had available to them, and destroying any hope of salvation except through a guilt-riddled concept of original sin, with women being the root of evil.

The information we study now survived only through the indescribable courage of brave souls in every generation who risked their lives to carry the knowledge from one place, one village, or one community to another.

Luckily for the world, the Grand Inquisitors in their eradication campaign did not believe in the concept of reincarnation. During the Roman Council of Nicea in 325 CE, all of the priests were gathered to share the writings they had collected about their religion in order to form the Roman Christian Church. These books were looked over and any of them that were considered to pose a problem for the Roman Empire in its campaign to dominate people and countries were thrown out. Priests who argued with the council and insisted that their religious texts be included were killed. The rest of the texts were burned and any remaining copies from the priests' homelands were destroyed. The concept of reincarnation was originally included in these texts but was reportedly removed by request of Empress Theodora, wife of Emperor Justinian in Constantinople.

Again, overwhelmingly brave people risked everything—including their families and their lives—to save copies of the ancient texts.

Many of these are now being restored and released, such as the Dead Sea scrolls and the Nag Hammadi library. One of the most interesting of these ancient ideas comes from teachings that existed thousands of years earlier and are still taught in Eastern philosophies: the concept of reincarnation.

The Grand Inquisitors' new religion held that you were given only one lifetime to live on Earth. It was easy for them to believe that if they simply killed the people who knew the ancient ways or who would not convert, they would solve the problem and eradicate the information for all time. However, the cycle of life, death, and rebirth (reincarnation) is alive and real, and those who were killed for sharing the ancient teachings and the power of the body/mind/spirit connection carried this information in their auric fields and akashic records. They returned back to the earthly plane, lifetime after lifetime, to remind people that they are greater than they remember or believe themselves to be. These brave souls return each generation to continue their work with this knowledge carried within them.

The Body/Mind/Spirit Reconnection

Now, in the twenty-first century, the tides are beginning to turn. Many doctors, scientists, and researchers are looking into the concept of the body/mind/spirit connection and opening up to the philosophy and practice of energy medicine. One of the true visionaries and pioneers of this process is Dr. C. Norman Shealy, the world's leading expert in pain and stress management. Shealy teaches and has written many books on the body/mind/spirit connection in the healing process, including *Life Beyond 100*.

So many metaphysical phenomena have been documented over the years that they can no longer be disregarded by the medical community. These include:

- Ongoing spontaneous remissions of cancer with no logical explanation.

- Patients with a positive outlook in life who experience quicker recovery rates and require less pain medication.

- Studies of patients who recovered more successfully than other similar patients when the only difference in the study was that their recovery was being prayed for by others.

- Patients who are cured from disease only to have it return again, even when, from all logical standpoints in the physical body, it should be healed.

- Powerful effects and changes in the body, such as lower heart rates and stabilized blood pressure levels, resulting from engaging in yoga and meditation.

- Research into and use of Eastern techniques—such as acupressure, reflexology, massage, and new techniques such as Healing Touch and EFT (emtional freedom techniques)—with successful results.

- Revealing out-of-body experiences (OBEs) and near-death experiences (NDEs) reported by a variety of patients, including doctors and nurses.

The number of people who are interested in alternative or complementary medicine is growing substantially. As a result, this movement has motivated the medical community to consider the idea of body/mind/spirit medicine. The outlook is hopeful that the Western world may again return to an age of healing where all parts of the person are engaged in the healing process.

In ancient times, it was easy to engage in energy medicine and natural healing. Many areas provided financially for temples to be built to house and provide for these types of healers. It was considered to be a necessary part of life and well-being, and the healers were a firmly established, well-known, and respected part of the community. Even in small villages, healers were provided for and cared for by the local residents.

Now people are being reintroduced to the practice of energetic techniques for healing. The holistic systems and procedures are not quite as organized yet as they were in the past, but they are making tremendous leaps. It's an exciting time for the future of humanity as science and spirituality begin to work together to explore the body/mind/spirit connection. I believe that we will soon see great advancements in this work.

Ancient Traditions to Restore the Auric Field

There are seven ancient traditions to restoring the auric field. They were used in ancient practices and are still effective today. I share these practices with students who study with me and when I teach and lecture in workshops. While it is extremely rare to find a healing temple that will focus on this type of healing these days, it is my dream to build one in this lifetime according to the ancient techniques and wisdom.

Sleep and Dream Interpretation

After you arrived at a healing temple and met with a team of metaphysicians to create a healing plan, you would go to sleep. While you slept in the healing temple room, a healer would watch over you and care for you. If you awoke during the night, they would be there to ask you to describe what you were dreaming, and they wrote it down. In the morning when you awoke, they would ask you again about your dreams. You would begin each morning by discussing your dreams and thoughts with them. This process would continue each night as you underwent your treatments at the temple. Throughout the healing session, whether it was days or weeks, you would meet with a team of healers who would work with you to interpret your dreams and help you understand what your higher self was communicating to you through your dreams.

Flowers and Herbal Teas

The study of flowers and herbs was once an ancient practice that was popular and well understood. Each flower is connected to an essence that heals the auric fields. Once the patient met with the team and treatments were prescribed, one of the first introductions of treatment to the patient was drinking specific concoctions of herbal teas and elixirs; fresh flowers were also used in a variety of treatments. The present-day practice of aromatherapy is derived from these healing techniques. Aromatherapy is extremely beneficial in the healing of the auric fields. Also, fresh flowers are required for some treatments in order to bring the essence directly from the flower for the work. The last vestige we see of this tradition in modern-day society is the practice of bringing or sending flowers to a person who is in the hospital as a "get well" gesture.

Energy Work

The patient was exposed to a wide variety of healing techniques, all of which incorporated energy work on the physical and spiritual levels. Much of this work began in a pool of water. The ancient Roman baths are the best examples of what these pools looked like: indoors, surrounded by stone, with warm fires going around the pool and plenty of areas to relax, recline, and drift off to sleep after leaving the water. A pool of water carries vibration and energy well, and when you immerse the patient in a pool of water, all of the auric bodies are engaged and open to the energy being directed.

I conduct this type of practice with students on a regular basis. Not only does energy work in the water allow for healing to occur, it also enhances the auric fields in order to raise the vibration of each field and heighten intuitive abilities.

Many other healing modalities of energy work were included in the regimen, including massage with prescribed aromatherapy oils and auric body energy work as trained priestesses worked to remove and clear negative energy and nonphysical beings from the fields.

Light and Color

A variety of rooms were built in the temples, some with full sunlight and others as dark as a cave with only lamps to give light. The intensity of light was prescribed according to what type of disease or illness the patient was suffering from. Many times during the treatments, the patient would gradually be moved from one room to another, as their energy and mood lifted and was restored. Color was also used in each of the rooms to affect the auric bodies. Patients were assigned specific colors of bedding to sleep on, their rooms were decorated in specific colors, and the robes they were given to wear were of specific colors. Treatments were designed incorporating clothing, food, flowers, and other elements to stimulate the chakras as well as the auric bodies.

Crystals and Gemstones

Energy work with crystals and gemstones was an integral part of the healing process. Energy workers included them in their treatments with massage and other energy practices, and many beds and walls in treatment rooms were surrounded with crystals and gemstones used in healing techniques. Cups and bowls were also made from gemstones and used for imbibing specific drinks and foods.

A piece of jewelry would be created for each patient, with specific gemstones and crystals for them to wear during healing energy work and after they left the temple. Prescriptive bags were also created for each patient using powerful concoctions made from mixtures of herbs, oils, and gemstones that the person would carry with them and inhale to bring the energy into their auric fields, both during treatments and later when they returned to their homes.

Sound Therapy

Crystal bowls, bells, and chimes were used throughout the healing process. Some of the sound was used in conjunction with the water treatments in the pools, since the vibration would travel deep throughout the water. The power of sound and light in healing practices is still not as completely understood as it was once in the ancient temples. Musical tones are very effective in healing the auric fields and raising their vibrations, as well as in helping to remove negative energy.

Food

A specific dietary regimen was assigned to each patient during their time at the healing temples. Fruits, vegetables, grains, and other essential oils and nutrients were planned for each meal according to what the patient needed in their treatment. The meals focused on cleansing the physical body as a detox as well as bringing in specific foods to enhance the chakras and restore vitality and energy to the auric fields.

Modern Steps to Restore the Auric Field

You don't have to go to a temple to restore your auric fields. Here are some techniques you can use today:

Step One: Identify the Problem

Let's begin by assessing the basic root of how a problem forms. By nature and design, we experience emotions, and some of them are negative and cause the reaction of fear. Because feeling fearful causes us to feel powerless, it creates negative energy. No one enjoys feeling negative emotions, so we subconsciously find a way to avoid the experience. For many people, the best shield they can think of is to subconsciously place a hard exterior around themselves, first their body, then their mind with rigid beliefs, and finally their soul by giving the appearance of being strong and in control.

Once a person creates this tough exterior, they feel they are safe and have created a barrier so nothing can reach them. They are correct— nothing can reach them, bad or good! By building these walls, they have imprisoned themselves. Very little energy flows in and very little energy moves outward. The aura responds to this lack of energy and focused thought of a barrier and hardens into a thick shell.

What is the long-term effect of hardening the aura? As it toughens and hardens, the aura dries up and cracks. The effect is similar to skin when it becomes dry. The aura is normally strong but supple, like the skin. A cracked aura results from an auric field that has become hardened; as it receives less and less energy (nourishment), it dries up and cracks. This leads the auric shield to become fragile and easily flake off and break apart. In this weakened state, large holes are open in the auric field, allowing emotions like anger, repression, worry, and depression to reach in and further penetrate all the bodies. In addition, creating a hardened auric field presents a tremendous obstacle to spiritual growth. The wall blocks energy and information from the higher realms and further distances the person from the source of energy. It has the unpleasant side effect of enhancing fear as it begins to crack, causing the person to retreat further inward, caught in a delusional state where they are convinced that they really are protecting themselves.

Step Two: Restore Energy

Healing of the auric fields has to begin within. Only the person who has built the wall can undo it. In order to do so, the first step is to find the courage to move out of fear and back into engaging in experiences, even with the knowledge that some experiences will be painful.

The second step is to think of others. When the energy is being expended into creating a protective shell, the emphasis is on self-protection and self-preservation. The focus is "me, me, me." In order to break free from this shell, the person has to think of others and want to give freely, without thought of compensation or fear or repercussions. When their thoughts turn to others, they are not focused on themselves all the time, as they were previously. They are no longer self-absorbed.

Step Three: Release Memories and Imprints

The third step is to forgive and forget. If the person continues to carry the memories of previous transgressions, they are constantly reliving the experiences and the pain associated with the event. Each time they think about what happened previously, they are creating thought forms and sending energy to the thought forms. Those thought forms only know how to do one thing, which is to remind the person of this fearful energy so they can create even more protective walls around themselves. This is a negative cycle that will perpetuate until it is actively destroyed. When the person can forgive and forget, they lift the energy and move it out of the auric fields, and the negative thought forms are destroyed at the same time.

Step Four: Raise Your Vibration
The fourth step is to practice raising the auric field energy through the exercise in chapter five to bring in new white light energy to restore the auric fields. Daily practice of bringing in new energy with positive thoughts and emotions—while removing old negative thoughts, emotions, and energy—will restore the auric fields. It is important to remember that it took a great deal of time and energy to build these walls and it will take time to restore new energy and rebuild healthy fields.

The human aura provides a direct connection to your soul. In these fields, love and fear cannot exist together. Love is the greatest power that exists, but energetically it cannot reside in the same space as fear. As powerful creators, we choose which energy we allow to reside in our auric fields. The choice is yours, so choose wisely. If you want to raise the vibration in each of your auric fields to its highest potential, there is a simple formula to do so: **radiate love in all your activities, emotions, thoughts, words, actions, and deeds.**

Restoring a Spongy and Soggy Auric Field

The auric fields are in a constant cycle of gathering energy, manifesting that energy according to thoughts and emotions, and moving it into and out of the physical body. The energy of the auric fields is what each person detects when meeting another person. We have created descriptions alluding to this fact. When we feel something overwhelmingly in our own auric system, we get goose bumps on our skin. When we attempt to describe feeling the auric energy of another, we include positive phrases such as "you really shine" or "just being in your presence makes me feel good." We also describe negative feelings we pick up on, such as "he gets under my skin" or "I wish I could break through the wall and see the real person inside." What you really mean is that you wish you could break through this person's auric field and reach their true emotional nature.

As we've discussed, when some people become overwhelmed physically, emotionally, and mentally, they don't choose to build a hardened wall in the auric fields. Instead the fields just wear down with the overwhelming amount of emotional energy pouring in; the fields become soggy. This turns the normally pliable auric field into a condition that appears more like a sponge. It's damp and soggy, and holes appear in the field where energy leaks out. People with this type of auric field resemble vampires, because the spongy porous aura is reaching out to other energy fields, trying to gain energy to heal itself. They are so emotionally exhausted that they are not aware they are pulling on your energy fields. You may become aware of this fact yourself only after leaving their presence and then noticing that you feel worn out and fatigued after spending time with them. If they were to describe how they feel, they would most likely say that they feel completely let down by others or by life in general. If I could describe what this type of field looks like, I would say that it looks like when someone has been crying for a long time.

The key to repairing a soggy auric field is similar to repairing the hardened field. In this case, the person has to start within and dig deep to find a passion and zest for life. They must connect with something that gives them the will to live and find purpose in their activities. Once they have connected again with these two things, they must follow each of the steps listed under the hardened aura. Over time, the auric fields will stop leaking with an overabundance of emotional energy. This will stop the crying/leaking energy and allow the auric field to return to its normal pliable and healthy shape.

The Auric Field and Other Energy Fields

Over the years, as I've observed energetic patterns and shapes in the auric fields, I've also seen short energy bursts erupting from the body, similar to what occurs when the sun emits a solar flare. These energetic bursts are capable of disrupting electronics and are felt by other people who have intuitive ability and are sensitive to energy. Some people are aware of the energy they can build; for others, it is a complete surprise when it occurs.

In some cases, it is not a burst of energy that is created, but rather negative energy residue that has built up and is trapped within the aura and energy bodies and is not able to be released properly. Visualize a thunderstorm right before the rain is released from the clouds and you'll get the idea what this looks like in the human aura. The clouds are heavy and full, the energy gathers, and the air feels pregnant, ready for a release. If the conditions are not right and the rain is not able to gently fall, tumultuous weather patterns can occur with lightning and high winds. Energy blocked in the fields can cause similar disruptions as it seeks to be released.

The auric fields are receiving and emitting electrical impulses into and out of the body all the time. With our hectic lifestyles and fast-paced lives, we often aren't able to release pent-up energy, and it builds until it erupts outward to release. For some people, they release this in bursts of anger; others cry when the energy reaches a certain level. Some people release it with a nervous habit, such as twirling their hair, biting their nails, or having difficulty sitting still and always fidgeting. Children now have less time for physical exercise and are spending more time indoors rather than in nature; as a result, they are unable to release the pent-up energy in their auric fields. This may be why children today seem to have such short attention spans. They lack a natural, regular opportunity to release these excesses of psychic energy.

Rather than seeking a natural way to release this energy buildup, the Western world has turned to prescriptions to depress the energy. Kids take attention deficit drugs and adults take anxiety medications. I'm having a difficult time seeing how this is going to fix the issue in the long run. Physical exercise, time spent in nature, and emotional release cannot heal all of the issues of true hyperactivity and other problems, but it can help a great deal.

When I read a person's aura, it shows me what layers are holding residual energy patterns in the mental, emotional, physical, or higher levels. It is important to note that energy patterns building up in the aura are not only negative. The potential is there to build up both negative and positive energy patterns. I build up energy patterns in my auric fields to use for creative endeavors in my work. This energy store allows me to accomplish a lot of things at the same time. It is a gift and, if used wisely, can be extremely helpful. It typically requires some instruction to learn how to build and cultivate this energy. This is what I teach as an esoteric wisdom teacher and describe as: "We are a sea of energy, floating in vibratory fields." Accessing these waves of energy consciously with practice and guidance can creative positive effects, including physical healing, soul healing, working with magic and nature, and raising the energy vibration of other people and places, no matter where they are in the world.

Some people who are connected to their intuitive abilities have not learned how to release the energy they take in from other energy fields around them. Instead, they have a tendency to release this pent-up energy in a large wave, which I refer to as an *energy blast.* This wave or blast affects the environment around them. If you are wondering if you are one of these people, I can give you a quick example to consider.

If you have ever found that lights go off or turn on when you walk or drive down the street, then you are one of these people who release energy in a blast or wave. If you have an overabundance of energy that is trying to release itself from the containment area of the auric fields, it can affect lights and other electronics as it is being released. Think of it as an electrical surge.

Many people are not aware of the energy they are releasing, and so it comes as a surprise when an electronic device is affected. Typically, they are releasing this energy when they are agitated or in a high emotional state (whether that's positive or negative). When the energy blast is released, it can affect the performance of radios, clocks, watches, computers, and televisions, or cause lights, security alarms, and other electronics in their vicinity to turn off and on repeatedly.

Parapsychological Research on the Phenomenon

There are a variety of physical, emotional, and spiritual reasons for energy blasts. For some, it occurs only when their emotions are running very high; for others, it was a random event occurring only when they were going through puberty. Some of these people are tapping into what is described in parapsychology as psychokinesis/telekinesis (PK/TK). While there are skeptics who will say that the human body is not capable of affecting these fields, those who have experienced doing so firsthand have seen the results.

There has been some scientific parapsychological research on this subject, including what is referred to as the Pauli effect, where technical equipment and machines randomly and intermittently fail to work around certain people. More research needs to be continued on psychokinesis, expanded consciousness, and expanded energy fields so that it can be further understood. Unfortunately, there has not been enough support with funding for many institutes to continue these studies at the level needed to provide the deeper research needed. Some of the most notable researchers in this field of study include J. B. Rhine, Bill Roll, Dean Radin, Robert Jahn, and Roger Nelson.

A form of psychokinesis/telekinesis is featured in the George Clooney movie *The Men Who Stare at Goats,* which focused on the U.S. Army's research into psi abilities. Another example would be the fictional book (and film) by Stephen King, *Carrie,* which displayed an extreme and negative show of psi ability with PK/TK force.

What to Do When Experiencing an Energy Blast

When you experience an energy blast and find that you have disrupted electronic equipment, stop right away and ask yourself, "How am I feeling? What's on my mind right now?" Gather this information for a length of time and you will be able to discern what trigger or triggers set off your energy spikes.

The next time you find stress building in you, take a moment to step away and take a few deep breaths, pulling clear, cool air into your body, down into your lungs, and holding it there for a moment. Then release the air fully through your mouth and visualize the stress leaving your body through the air you are expelling. Repeat this three times and notice how different you feel. It won't take away the work and stressors you have at hand, but physically, you will feel more relaxed and able to tackle the situation or project without as much stress in your body and in your energy fields.

Over the past decade, I have seen people's energy fields expanding, and I believe we will begin to see greater activity within these fields, such as energy blasts and expressions, which some currently describe as paranormal activity. As we evolve as a species, more of these unsolved mysteries will become commonplace and considered to be a natural sixth sense rather than a supernatural one.

Meditation

The act of meditation is one of the most rewarding gifts you can give to yourself, yet the concept is daunting for many. There are those who enter into meditative practices that evolve into an entire lifestyle, but for those who have never tried to meditate, the idea of sitting in a potentially uncomfortable position in complete silence is enough to discourage even the most casual of attempts. If you are looking to adopt a meditation practice, begin by disregarding any preconceived notions of how you think a meditation practice should operate. The key to a successful meditation practice is to create a routine that feels right for you.

Here are some tips on how to create a meditative practice in order to balance your auric fields and bring focus and control to expressing energy from these fields:

One of the easiest ways is to adopt a simple ten-minute meditation, which I refer to as ten-minute bliss breaks. Create a set time that will become your ten-minute meditation time. Perhaps you'll wake early before the rest of your household to have those quiet ten minutes each day, or maybe you'll take them outside in a park during your lunch hour. Many people prefer to meditate in the evening to relax after a busy day and to open their mind to a deeper dream state. Crucial in any meditation practice is breathing. Regardless of whether you wish to spend ten minutes in meditation or ten hours, slow and deep methodical breathing will relax the body and bring oxygen to the lungs and bloodstream. It will also help you to retain focus and awareness.

When beginning a new meditation practice, you may find that it proves too difficult to simply relax and think of nothing for an entire ten minutes. Do not feel concerned—this is your practice and you can create a meditation ritual that feels right for you at this time. Your personal meditation routine will evolve over time as you continue the practice. In the beginning, just the slow, deep breathing is good for the body and will relax you.

For many people, guided meditations are a wonderful way to meditate. You can listen to the meditation on CD or on your MP3 player in your home or with headphones anywhere you are. Simply choose the meditation that appeals to you and enter the journey the guided meditation provides with a spoken script and relaxing music. Guided meditations allow your mind to focus on particular images, allowing for creative visualization and helping the mind to focus on the journey at hand rather than other distractions.

If your day is full and you don't have time for a guided meditation, create a sacred space for yourself that you can return to often. As you begin your meditation, picture a peaceful scene that you find relaxing. Perhaps it's the beach or a mountaintop or a lush garden. Try to remember your most peaceful moment and build from there. Create the scene in your mind, adding beautiful details. If you find a garden to be calming, add a bench where you will sit in the garden. See the trees and the cascade of flowers blooming in a multitude of colors. Listen for the sound of birds chirping and hear the soft breeze blowing through the trees. Tilt your head back and savor the warmth of the sun on your face. Breathe in slowly and deeply and exhale fully, releasing the air from deep within. Take your shoes off and sink your feet deep into the soft grass, flexing your toes. As you breathe in again deeply, smell the flowers as their scent fills the garden. Now, if you wish, you can release whatever is troubling you. You may choose to ask that a guide or friend come to sit with you on the bench to listen to you as you share your thoughts and concerns. You might create a lake around the garden or a waterfall to swim in. As you swim, you release your cares and watch them float away and dissolve. Perhaps a pet from your childhood joins you in the garden and you spend time with them, petting and playing with them, forgetting your cares of the day.

Continue building this place in great detail each day during your ten-minute meditation and visualization until you can see it fully in your mind and know it well. Then claim this scene as your sacred space. Know that you can return there anytime—all you need to do is to sit quietly, breathe deeply, and imagine this scene in your mind. In this space, you can relax and spend a few minutes away from the world. Once you have created a meditation practice, you can then work with guided meditations—or a creative visualization meditation of your own making—to send energy to your auric fields and chakras. You can also use deep breathing techniques to release old energy and bring new energy into each of the fields.

This act of active meditation can become a profound spiritual practice that can have a significant impact on your day, creating a sense of relaxation and well-being and restoring vitality, energy, and creativity to the auric fields and chakra system.

Eight

SENSING THE ENERGY FIELD IN BUILDINGS AND IN THE LAND

If there be righteousness in the heart, there will
be beauty in the character. If there is beauty in the
character, there will be harmony in the home. If
there is harmony in the home, there will be order
in the nation. When there is order in each nation,
there will be peace in the world.

—Chinese proverb

Every living thing has an energy field surrounding it that generates the life force. While humans have their own personal energy fields, organic material on Earth resonates with a planetary energy field, which connects to the elements of nature—earth, air, fire, and water—and to the eight directions—north, south, east, west, northeast, northwest, southeast, and southwest.

The land is also affected by the energy of ley lines (natural Earth energy lines, similar to meridians), which connect with water running underground and energy portals located in certain parts of the world. When two different ley lines intersect, the energy is intensified; depending on the types of energies that are connecting, this can lead to an overwhelmingly positive space or a very negative space. These energetic hot spots are frequently used as sites for religious buildings, such as temples, churches, and sanctuaries.

Each area of the world has a specific energy created in part by the natural elements and elementals nurturing it. Some are bursting with natural energy and vitality while others have been depleted by overfarming, famine, and drought and are still in a process of recovering their vital energy and natural resources. Other parts of the world have seen so many wars and conflicts that the energy has been drowned in the sorrow of it all. The Earth has a natural capability to heal itself, and over time it will do so, but it takes many decades and in some cases centuries to recover from serious trauma. When looking for the most nurturing place for you and your family to live, it is wise to take all of this information into account. A home built on land that is not at rest will not feel comfortable and welcoming.

Eastern Auric Field Philosophy: The Art of Feng Shui

One of the most widely recognized traditions of connecting people with the energy of their dwellings and the land on which they sit is the art of Feng Shui. Traditional Feng Shui began almost six thousand years ago in China and continues today, using geomancy, time, space, energy, and nature to create good health, harmony, and positive energy in private homes and commercial buildings. Each structure is designed and complemented by the interior decor in order to create balance for people in conjunction with their surrounding environment. The natural surroundings around each structure have great importance and must be taken into consideration, since they greatly affect the energy in the home or building. This includes the direction the building faces; the locations of water, mountains, and other landscape features; and the surrounding buildings and other structures.

The building itself has a birth date, which is when the roof is attached to the walls and the structure is enclosed. From this date forward, the home begins to capture and store energy, beginning with the natural surroundings that affect it, including the amount of light it receives, whether or not it is close to water, if it is overshadowed by taller buildings, sits on a ley line, or is surrounded by trees and mountains. Some building materials continue to reverberate with their own energy after they are pulled from their natural surroundings and introduced into the home, such as hardwoods, granite, and stone. This is a lot to consider, but there are even more elements that affect the overall energy of the home or workspace.

Traditional Feng Shui takes into account the birth date of each person and determines whether they are an east energy or a west energy and how this will affect them in regard to the energy of the home. Just as we look at the astrological chart of a person when they are born, traditional Feng Shui looks at the birth chart of the home, and time is an important factor here. Each year, a new chart is drawn up for the home, since the space's energy shifts and changes just as it does in a person's astrological chart. When the Feng Shui of the home and land is understood, along with the astrological charts of each person residing in the home, it provides opportunities for greater peace and harmony in the home and new ways to maximize this for each person. Consulting with a traditional Feng Shui expert can provide great insight into the planetary energy fields and ley lines surrounding your home or office, as well as the energy residing inside your building. It will also provide some guidance and input into feelings you may already be having about the energy in your home or office.

Auric Energy Fields

Each area of the world has its own unique energy and auric field. Mountainous areas give off one type of energy, which varies significantly from the energy of beach areas. As I travel, I can't help but notice the aura of each region. Some areas radiate with the color so intensely that it fills the sky.

One example that has always stayed with me are landscapes and seascapes painted by artists who portrayed an overwhelming shade of pink throughout the canvas. These seascapes were always connected with Florida, but I never really understood why the artist would choose to use so much pink in their painting of a blue ocean and beige sand. I surmised that they must have been trying to capture the glow of a sunset at that brief moment when the sky turns pink. Years later, when I was moving to Florida, I experienced what these artists were putting in their paintings. When driving into the state, there's a certain demarcation line where the auric field in the land and sky turns pink! I was overcome by the beauty of it, and I realized why so many people are drawn to live in Florida—for the healing heart energy they receive while there. It truly is a wonderful place to heal and enhance the heart chakra area. Though I no longer live in Florida, I drive there often. When I do, I can now calculate to almost the exact mile where the energy changes and the pink glow begins. It is as thrilling to me each time I see the pink hue as it was the very first time.

Another powerful area with a strong auric energy is the Hawaiian islands. There are parts of Hawaii where the energy is so pure that you soak up the auric field through all of your five senses, and even the intangible sixth sense. Hawaii exudes the energy of "creative fire," and when you visit the islands, your creative energy will rise. It is rare to meet anyone who has spent time there who has not found that they return home energetically uplifted and inspired. Their auric field is recharged and full of light and vitality and is ready to create and manifest something new and exciting from the time they spent in the islands. If you are looking to make a change in your life and want to connect with your creativity and reignite that spark, a visit to Hawaii should be on your list of things to do.

Connect with Local Energy

Are you wondering what the energy is like where you live? You can learn to see the auric patterns in the land and around your home and office and be your own guide to choosing the right property for you. Let's begin with an exercise to connect you to the vibrational energy of planet Earth.

Exercise: Dowsing to Connect with Earth's Energy Fields

Dowsers are able to connect with Earth's energy lines and sense what is lying below the ground. Expert dowsers are able to locate underground water, oil, precious metals, and unmarked gravesites. Dowsing can be done using copper rods, simple metal rods, a pendulum, or two tree branches that are light enough to be held comfortably in your hand. Willow and witch hazel are two of the most popular branch choices for dowsing. Your selection of a dowsing tool should be a personal preference according to what feels most comfortable.

To begin dowsing, hold a rod in each hand and walk slowly over an area of land. The rods should be held horizontally in your hands but not gripped tightly; they should be allowed to move and shift. Focus on what you are looking for, whether it is to connect with one of Earth's ley lines, or to find water, oil, metal, or bone. When you encounter an underground area that resonates energetically with the item you are searching for, the rods will move toward each other and cross to form an *X*.

During the act of dowsing, you are expanding your auric field outward to connect and merge with the auric field of Earth. You create a focused thought in your auric field, asking it to search and connect with the energy of the target you have in mind. To find water, for example, you are transmitting—through your auric fields—the connection you wish to establish with the energy of the field of water below the ground. You are putting out a call in order to connect with the energy field produced by water and ignoring all other energy patterns and fields. The energy field of the planet responds to this request and, as you near an area where the energy of water is present, the field responds to your request and communicates this through your auric fields. This information is then transferred to the divining rods in your hands, signaling that water is near.

Many dowsers find that, with practice, they no longer need to use a rod, wand, or pendulum at all. Over time, they connect with their intuitive side and tap directly into their auric fields to receive the message directly, including through their hands as a form of psychometry or through their third-eye perception.

Connect with and Change the Energy in Your Home

In the principles of Feng Shui, one of the most basic and important "cures" (a correction to adjust the energy in a space) is to restore order and calm by the removal of clutter from the home. This simple act can create an immediate visually and emotionally uplifting effect, allowing energy or chi to circulate fully throughout the room. By simply removing the overwhelming stimuli (clutter), a more peaceful and healthy environment is created.

Many people perform this task through the ritual of spring and fall cleaning. During this process, the home is cleaned extensively after a long, cold winter or hot summer when the windows and doors remained closed, preventing fresh air from circulating freely throughout the house.

Cultural groups, past and present, celebrate the seasons as powerful cycles of change, revering the concept that what occurs in nature also occurs within man. Again we come back to "As Within, So Without," meaning that how we think and feel radiates outward in how we act and live. The act of removing clutter in the home can also remove energetic clutter in the mental and emotional fields.

In my book *9 Life Altering Lessons*, I discuss the energy of our words and the significant impact they create in the home.

> *... Energy does not die, it just changes form. In the same respect, words do not die. Picture your home for a moment. Once you have the image of your home in mind, think about what conversations (words) occurred in your home in the past year. The energy in words, have a sticky substance to them. They attach themselves to people, places and things, especially in homes, which hold energy as we spend so much time indoors, especially during the fall and winter months.*

> *Take a moment and imagine that you are holding a blue light, similar to what is used in crime scenes to detect invisible stains, which cannot be viewed with the naked eye. Shine this blue light on the walls of your home and visualize every word spoken in your home during the past year. Energetically, all of these words are stuck on the walls of your home, like wallpaper and each of them radiate energy, which reflects off of your walls. Ask yourself, what kind of energy has been created in my home?*

Exercise: Cleansing Residual Energy in Your Home

To remove residual energy, here are four steps to cleanse and restore the energy in your home in order to provide a healthy environment for the body, mind, and spirit of all who live or spend time there.

Step One: Create a ceremonial cleansing ritual in your home, using white sage to smudge and purify each room (check with your local metaphysical store to obtain instructions on how to properly use white sage). Make sure to say a prayer of protection when you begin. As you move throughout your home purifying the rooms with the sage, say aloud a prayer or mantra to bless and clear each room of your home. Open the windows in each room during this ritual to send the old energy outdoors to be dispersed. If your home has been exposed to more intense emotions and arguments for a prolonged period of time, you may need to repeat this ritual several times over the course of the year to completely remove the residual energy.

Step Two: Paint the walls in a room where you would like to completely change the energy. Select an entirely different color for your walls and ask for guidance to choose the color most needed in this room. You can also refer to the home décor suggestions in chapter four for the effects of some paint colors.

After using sage to purify the room, play uplifting music while painting. As you begin to paint, take a section of the wall and say the word aloud that you would like the room to energetically align with, such as *love, peace, or grace.* With your paintbrush, lightly paint the word on the wall while saying it aloud three times. Be sure to quickly roll fresh paint over the word before it dries, otherwise the word will bleed through when the paint dries. If you are painting several rooms, you may wish to create special words for each room. Words that describe an emotion work best, such as *abundance* in the dining room, *peace* in a child's room, *love* in the master bedroom, and *divine order* in an open/communal space to set the intention for the entire home.

Step Three: Once the paint has dried and the room is put back together, the addition of fresh flowers is the quickest way to bring in positive new energy to the home. Think of your home as a sacred temple, and keep it free from clutter, both in the physical and metaphysical senses, as clutter can have a detrimental effect on the energy of the room and the people who inhabit the space.

Step Four: Purchase decorative lettering to apply to the wall. There are many companies offering a variety of inspirational quotes, or you can create a custom phrase of your own. With an empowering phrase in your room as a visual accent, the new intention and direction for the home is clearly stated.

For Added Effect: To create an energetic boost in your room, purchase ground quartz as sold in the paint department of home renovation stores, which is specially designed to go into the paint. Before mixing the quartz into the paint, hold the bag of quartz in your hands and direct positive energy and intentions into it. Mix the quartz into the paint thoroughly while stating your intentions and positive affirmations. Go on to paint the room as described here. The end result will reflect both your thoughts and energy as well as create a beautiful sheen on the walls.

Exercise: Sensing the Aura of Your Home or Workplace

Once you have begun practicing seeing auras, it becomes easier to sense the auric fields in other objects. You may develop abilities with psychometry, where you are able to hold an object and detect energy imprints that have attached to the object, such as holding an old watch and sensing the energy of the person who wore the watch each day. You may also find that you have a stronger connection with gemstones and crystals, and resonate with their energy and want to work with them further.

As we discussed previously, a home will hold energy, and unless it is cleared and cleaned, it will continue to resonate with the energy it receives on a daily basis. When looking to purchase a new property or rent a home or office, it is very helpful to sense the energy in the building, so you can determine whether or not the energy of the space will be nurturing for you, your family, or your work environment.

There are several ways to sense the energy of a building. Below are just two examples of how to do so. Try them and see which you strongly connect with in order to determine the right practice for you. As you continue to work on your abilities with auras, you may also develop your own practice for sensing the energy of places.

Intuitive ability is like every other ability—some days you are at your highest peak of power and other days are just "off" days. This is just like a power hitter in baseball at the top of his game who is still susceptible to days when, try as he might, he doesn't hit the ball. If you need to discern the energy in the room on one of these days and your intuitive ability is clouded for any reason, there are other ways to reveal the energy in a room. The first is to place a crystal glass in the middle of the room on a table. Fill the glass with bottled water, preferably from a bottle that you have brought with you from another location. Leave the glass of water sitting on the table and take the rest of the bottled water with you. While waiting, walk around another part of the house and attempt to sense any energy disruptions in the home on your own. After ten minutes, return to the table where the glass of water was placed and sit down. Take out the bottle of water you carried with you and take a drink. Be aware of how the water tastes in your mouth. Wait for a moment and then take a drink of water from the crystal glass. If there is a noticeable discrepancy between the bottled water and the water from the glass, there is a high probability of an energy disruption in the home.

Another method is to enter the home or office when it is completely quiet and no one else is inside the building. Walk from room to room, spending a few minutes in each. While in each room, stand quietly, clear your mind, and ask the room to "speak" to you. Relax, close your eyes if you are comfortable doing so, and allow the energy of the room to connect with you. As your intuitive abilities increase, you'll detect energy imprints in the room and can pick up on people who have lived there as well as any expressive or volatile emotions that were released in the room. One side effect of connecting with homes and offices this way is that if you also possess mediumship abilities, ghosts who are still attached to the land, buildings, or even antique furniture in the home may reach out to communicate with you.

For this reason, I am very particular about having antiques in my home. I normally refrain from buying antiques, as many of them carry old emotional energy and baggage with them, which then radiates in your home when you bring them in. I have only a few antique pieces, and these were carefully selected because they exude a high imprint of loving energy that can still be felt today.

If you have conducted the exercise and find that the home you are looking to purchase or rent has residual negative energy, follow the steps from the painting exercise to clear residual energy from the home upon moving in. Along with the white sage treatment, you can also sprinkle sea salt along the windowsills and doorjambs to seal in the new energy and repel negative energy.

In most cases, these exercises will take care of clearing the energy in the home. If you encounter a home that radiates a very strong negative vibration, these exercises may not be strong enough to fix the problem at hand. Depending upon what occurred in the house, the energy memory or imprint may be very strong and could take years or even decades to restore.

You would then need to make the decision as to whether this is the type of energy you would want to be surrounded by for that period of time. For most people, the cons of this situation outweigh the pros, and the property should be avoided.

Nine

CONNECTING WITH THE AURA THROUGH THE NATURAL ELEMENTS

The art of healing comes from nature, not from the physician. Therefore the physician must start from nature, with an open mind.

—Paracelsus

The elements of nature provide tremendous resources, including opportunities to connect with each of the elements to assist in healing and restoring energy to the auric fields. The uplifting sights, vibrational sounds, and revitalizing scents of nature's finest renew the mind, body, and spirit on multiple levels. In addition, the seasonal cycles connect us to Earth-based energetic transformations.

When we understand how to connect with the cycles, we can draw upon their energy to further enhance our auric bodies, and when we focus our energy in conjunction with the elements, we can create forces of powerful healing energy. These forces are the most powerful during seasonal cycles on Earth; when we harness this energy and draw it into our fields, the energy magnifies threefold. The cycles represent the physical stages of life each person goes through—the spring of our youth, the summer peak of our adult years, the reaping of wisdom in our golden years of autumn, and our death and return to the spirit world in winter.

In this chapter, we'll discuss how to connect with the natural forces and elements of our planet. Each season presents powerful opportunities to enhance your auric energy using each element in nature while connecting with the seasonal cycles. The mental auric field can be best restored in the fall, the physical auric field hibernates and replenishes energy in the winter, spring stimulates and activates the astral auric field and the heart chakra, and the emotional auric field is revitalized in the light of summer. Note that any date references given here are for the Northern Hemisphere; if you live in the Southern Hemisphere, simply adjust the timing to match the natural seasons in order to reach the desired effect.

You can choose among the exercises whether you simply wish to connect with the natural forces to restore your energy, or if you wish to go further and engage actively with the natural resources in order to draw more energy into your auric fields.

Connecting to the Energy of Earth and the Season of Fall

After experiencing periods of prolonged stress, the auric field can become depleted. Depending on what exactly has occurred in the mental, emotional, and physical auric fields, it can take months and sometimes years for the fields to fully recover. These are the situations when you need to fully restore and repair the auric field.

In these cases, it is important to rebuild the aura at the foundation. Working with earth energy grounds our physical body, connects us back to our etheric auric field, and supports the root chakra. What follows are some ways to connect with earth energy.

Dig in the Soil: Working in a garden is one of the best ways to stimulate the necessary recovery process. Begin by kneeling on the ground and digging a hole in the soil. As you dig, remove old roots and obstacles in order to prepare a healthy space for what you are going to plant. The "hands-on" contact with the soil connects your physical body to your auric field, and the kneeling position opens the root chakra area, allowing it to release pent-up energy. In this position, the chakras in the sole of the feet are also exposed and release energy into the ground. Using your hands, place the seed or bulb into the hole. When covering the hole, use your bare hands so that you establish direct contact with the soil, as this allows the chakras in the hands to connect with the earth and release energy. As this process is repeated, the healing occurs without having to be consciously aware of it happening. Gardening in this manner is healing on all levels and is especially good for children who need to release stress.

An Earth-Based Ritual

Timing is everything, and when you understand (as our ancient ancestors did) that there are certain days of the year on which energy can be magnified, it can be a tremendous boost to working with and enhancing your auric fields, which in turn can help manifest your dreams and goals.

In the Western world, we set new goals during the New Year's celebration of January 1. Energetically, this is a difficult time to stimulate energy, since it is in the dead of winter, when nature and our bodies are in hibernation mode. To connect with the energy of nature, the time to create new resolutions is in the fall. In the fall, we go "back to school." Our mental field is the most active and engaged, and we buckle down to work. In the garden, we till the soil and plant seeds and bulbs, giving them time to germinate underground through the winter so they can sprout forth and bloom in the spring.

When we make a resolution and plant that seed of thought in the dead of winter on January 1, there is little warmth and light to nurture these thoughts. It is no surprise that many New Year's resolutions are dead and gone only a few weeks into the year, as there was no nourishment for the seeds to take hold.

The season of fall energetically represents the time for seeds of thought to be planted in our mental auric field in order to give them contemplation and introspection. When we create our goals in the fall for the coming year, we have the season of winter to mull them over and build a powerful action plan for spring, when energy is at its peak.

Exercise: Create a Symbolic Seed-Planting Tradition in the Fall

Invite friends to gather and celebrate the New Year on October 31 or November 1, which in ancient times for the Celts was celebrated as the New Year. (This also coincides with the Wiccan holiday of Samhain, which signals the beginning of a new turn on the Wheel of the Year.) Hand out a piece of paper to each person at the gathering and ask everyone to write down their resolution. Then take turns reading them aloud to the group to share everyone's hopes and dreams. During this time, the group offers their encouragement and blessings. As each person finishes reading aloud their dreams, a candle is lit for them and a toast with juice, water, or wine is given.

Important Note: Pay particular attention to what you drink and toast to around Halloween, for with each glass you raise in a toast, the energy will be heightened. This is a time when the energy fields and the Veil between the earthly plane and the spirit worlds are wide open. This creates a rare opportunity to manifest your desires by imbuing into the liquid what you are thinking and saying as you make each toast. You truly can activate your libations with your energy, turning them into powerful potions, which you then drink and absorb into your auric fields.

Next, hand out packages of seeds along with little clay pots filled with soil and invite your guests to plant new seeds of thought this fall to manifest in the spring. Have each person write one word that describes the goal they wish to manifest on the outside of their clay pot. A permanent marker works best for this purpose.

On January 1, celebrate the conventional New Year with a toast to your dreams. They have been actively manifesting for several months now in your mental auric field and will soon be ready for action in the outer world this coming spring.

Mountain Energy

Each mountain range holds a specific type of energy. There is a saying in Asheville, North Carolina: "altitude affects attitude." The Blue Ridge Mountains in North Carolina are very old and rounded and exude a soft feminine energy. The quartz level is very high in these mountains, and the quartz radiates the energy that it receives from within the ground and from the people who live near the range. This is in large contrast to the Rocky Mountains in Colorado, which are angular and exude a strong masculine energy. The Blue Ridge Mountains connect with Divine Feminine energy and bring peace and stillness. They would be considered to be yin (passive), while the Rocky Mountains connect with Divine Masculine energy and would stimulate action and drive with their yang (action) energy.

Another example is the islands of Hawaii with their volcanic energy, which stimulates rebirth and creative energy. The type of restorative energy you are seeking should be taken into consideration when choosing which mountain range to visit or, in some cases, live near for an extended period of time. It's important to choose the right setting to help rebalance the fields that need restorative energy. For example, if you are very passive and have lost the will to get things done and take action, connecting with a passive energy area will not help stimulate your energy fields. Often we have to get out of our comfort zone in order to get back into balance. Once we are back in balance, we can return to live in the environment we naturally find most harmonious.

Crystals and Gemstones

Crystals and gemstones are gifts from earth energy and serve as wonderful tools when working with our auric fields. In order to do significant clearing and restoring of the auric fields, the size of the crystal or gemstone is important. A small crystal cannot radiate or absorb enough energy to fully clear the fields. In most cases, the stone needs to be as large as the palm of the hand. In some cases, several crystals of this magnitude may be required to repair the field. Crystals and gemstones are meant to work in conjunction with other healing techniques when repairing or clearing the auric fields. An example would be when an energy worker or healer uses crystals on and around the body they are working on while also removing and clearing the energy around the person.

Connecting to the Energy of Water and the Season of Winter

Water is the most healing and magnifying element of them all for the auric fields. Each time we take a shower or bath, we are able to remove and clear residual energy and restore our body and auric fields. Spending time in a pool where one can do prolonged energy work in water is highly recommended and can rebalance and expand the auric fields to a great degree.

If you can also connect the pool with a water feature, as seen in many swimming pools now with a waterfall, this creates negative ionic energy, similar to waves crashing on the beach, which is very good for the auric energy to absorb. Even on days when you are not in the pool, just sitting near the water is beneficial. If you don't have a pool, build a large waterfall in your backyard or buy the largest water fountain you can to create this sparkling energy.

Another option to draw in water energy is to install a rainfall showerhead in your shower. Once it is installed, sit directly under the rainfall and cup your hands together at the chest level. As you do so, the water will catch in your hands and splash, which simulates a waterfall. This is only a small way to create this energy, but it's still effective. Having access to a pool with a waterfall feature where you can truly be immersed is the best way to have this continuous energy around you and your home. The effect is uplifting for everyone in your home who uses the shower.

Nature creates this natural resource at the beach. When the waves crash onto the shore, it creates negative ions, which are the most beneficial natural element you can receive to bring full restoration, vitality, and enhanced growth to all of the fields. When I'm asked how best to recharge one's aura quickly, I always say, "Get thee to the beach!" There is no faster way currently known to heal the auric field. It has worked for me personally more times than I can count and still does.

Water is a powerful element to work with, since it can change from liquid to solid to gas. The ritual outlined for the Summer Solstice (see page 175) should also be used during the Winter Solstice. Both cycles represent the change from light to dark and dark to light, and complete the cycle of the year.

To stimulate the water energy around your auric fields on a daily basis, keep a water fountain in your home, in a room that you occupy each day or evening. Preferably the water fountain would be made from natural elements, such as slate or stone, and have stones at the base of the water fountain so that the water sprays on the rocks. Some people take this further with the addition of a saltwater aquarium in their home, which can be very peaceful—and the fish are quite beautiful to watch. If you consider having an aquarium over a fountain, salt water is preferred to represent the energy of the ocean.

Connecting to the Energy of Air and the Season of Spring

Few things excite my energy fields more than a good breeze when it picks up and I feel it swirling around me. A gentle breeze brings much more than cooling relief to the body, stimulating the energy fields and removing residual energy. A strong breeze, such as during a storm, electrifies this energy and, after blowing away stagnant energy, it stimulates the vibration of the fields. This is why many people become excited during a storm—it stirs something deep within and calls them into action.

When you need to remove residual energy from your auric fields and want a quick recharge, going somewhere with strong breezes will do the trick. A mountain area with strong breezes will work, as will an island that receives the trade winds. Traveling on a cruise ship also connects you with the ocean breeze. During the cruise, stand at the front of the ship and let the breeze blow over you. Doing this activity for a few minutes a day on a cruise ship will literally blow your cares away.

However, there are some occasions where the wind is not helpful in removing energy from the auric fields. Dry desert winds are not beneficial. An example of how dry wind affects people is the Santa Ana winds, which blow in Southern California. When the Santa Ana winds arrive, people report feeling nervous, uptight, or on edge and have strong mood swings and irritability. These winds carry a large number of positive ions. Negative ions provide a peaceful and calming effect to the human auric fields; the opposite occurs with positive ions, as they make people feel upset and uncomfortable. The overabundance of positive ions in the Santa Ana winds also disrupts the auric energy fields rather than enhancing them.

Take a Breath of Fresh Air: To clear energy from the auric fields, spend some time in an area with a strong breeze. To restore energy to the auric fields using the element of air, refer to the deep breathing and meditative exercises found throughout this book. Pull clear fresh air and pure energy into the auric fields using three deep breaths. Deep breathing exercises are beneficial to the physical body, and with each exhale you remove negative energy from the body and auric fields. To add air energy in or around your home, a wind chime will move the energy around your home. Place it near a window where a breeze will blow the chime around or near an air register where it will chime when the air conditioner or heating unit kicks in. If you prefer not to have a noisemaker near a window or vent, ring the wind chime once a day to circulate air energy.

Behold the Power of Spring

The mere mention of spring reminds me of a chance to begin everything in life anew. On a deeper level, I remember past lives as a Celtic maiden, playing hide and seek in the woods with friends and delighting in the discovery of a meadow of flowers, plucking a handful of them to make herbal concoctions and a potion or two for safekeeping.

Times have changed, and I (like most of us) live in an overly domesticated suburban world, with only small patches and parks to remind me of my natural roots. Yet, at the first signs of spring, my shoes go flying off and I have to sink my toes deep into the green grass to connect my auric fields back into nature.

One evening, while I was out doing just this very thing and a bit of stargazing, I was greeted by the sweetest little bunny in my yard. As I stood there in the quiet of my backyard, I felt a stirring from deep within me, heralding the return of my creativity, fertility, and sense of adventure. Above me the stars of my ancestors surrounded me with their love, reminding me that I never walk alone, and here next to me stood the goddess Ostara, represented in the form of this beautiful bunny, inviting me to embrace the Divine Feminine and take a walk on the wild side. Never one to turn down an invitation, I opened mind, heart, body, and soul and joined in on nature's dance for a few hours, reveling in the silver light of the moon.

The next morning, I reflected on the ritual known as spring break, and how the word *break* means to end one thing and begin something new. *Breakfast* for example, means to transition from being asleep and not eating to awakening and eating, thus "breaking the fast." In the same way, we follow a similar ritual with spring break, as we stir from the deep slumber of winter and emerge from hibernation and the cave of the home. In this sense we are like our ancestors, breaking from the cold bonds of winter and entering a new cycle. This is why rituals were created, to mark the passage of time and the movement from one season to another or to memorialize a special event or ceremony.

Spring is the most powerful time of the year to raise the vibration of all of the auric fields. The Spring Equinox is the best time of the year to raise the energy in the auric fields and chakras and open the heart chakra. As mentioned earlier, the heart chakra and astral field open when the lower bodies are clear and the energy is ready to rise. Like the flowers of spring, all good things bloom in time. Spring represents joy, hope, adventure, and love. It is a time to play. We are emerging from the restorative period of winter and are full of energy to express.

If you have planted the seeds of thought and affirmation in the fall, you will now be prompted from within on how best to take action at this time. Enjoy, for all of nature is with you at this time, bursting with color and vibrant energy. The world is a virtual feast of energy and your auric fields will soak it up every day. Throw open the windows, go on long walks, surround yourself with fresh flowers, and—best of all—go out and play.

Rather than a formal ritual for the Spring Equinox, it is preferable to let your heart be your guide and to receive inner intuitive guidance on how best to connect with the Spring Equinox energy. One good practice to follow is to begin with the deep cleaning of the home and purification of the body, as in the exercise on page 175. This will prepare you for the energy to come on the Spring Equinox.

Connecting to the Energy of Fire and the Season of Summer

The energy of fire has a purifying effect on the auric fields. The quickest and easiest way to connect with fire energy is to spend time basking in the sunlight, which restores vital energy.

The most powerful time of the year to connect with the elemental energy of fire is in June, during Midsummer and the Summer Solstice. The Summer Solstice is a three-day cycle of the apex of the sun's journey bringing light to Earth. Ancient Celts celebrated this event by lighting huge bonfires, called balefires, to keep the light around them for this entire period. People wore amulets made with herbs and charms to restore energy, while others danced around the balefires for purification, good health, and love.

Midsummer eve marks the end of the Summer Solstice and is a powerful time of transformation and purification through the element of fire. It is said that Divine Feminine energy manifests as Mother Earth and Divine Masculine energy manifests as the Sun King. Many cultures celebrate Midsummer by building giant bonfires to dance around beginning at dusk on June 23 and continuing until the sunrise on June 24 (these dates shift around a bit each year, however, as our calendar system is not 100 percent aligned with the astronomical forces).

The Veils between the earthly plane and the spirit planes are thinner during this three-day period. The evenings before, during, and after the Summer Solstice are an important time of the year to pay attention to your dreams. It is reported that what is dreamed of during this three-day period will come to fruition.

Fire Energy Purification Ritual for Summer Solstice

In my work as a wisdom teacher, I share rituals that were once used in ancient temples, transforming them into modern-day practices. The Summer Solstice is a powerful time to visualize any negative thoughts and energy burning away to nothingness.

Here is a purification/cleansing ritual for the Summer Solstice. This ritual is to be done the night before the Summer Solstice. On the day of the Summer Solstice, it is time to laugh, play, and do something joyful, as your energy has been cleansed and you are now going to soak up the rays of the sun and revitalize your auric fields.

Step One: Make a conscious decision that you are ready to remove any negative thoughts, emotions, and painful memories you have been holding on to. Begin by writing down your negative feelings on paper. Once you have created this list, read over what you wrote and make the conscious decision to forgive each transgression done to you. Declare to yourself that you are releasing the past and will no longer hold on to old memories that weigh you down. Further declare that you will no longer allow the past to affect your future. Light a small fire in a safe container and location and place your list into the fire. As the smoke rises from the burning paper, ask that your negative feelings and thoughts be removed from your auric fields and carried away by the smoke into the sky.

Step Two: Remove residual negative energy from your home. In order to do this, bundle rosemary and white sage together with red, black, and white thread and dip the tips into a bowl of spring water. Sprinkle the water around your house to remove negativity and cleanse and purify the space. The exercise shared in chapter eight on how to clear the energy from your home is also beneficial at this time.

Step Three: Purify and cleanse your body and auric fields. Take a shower and visualize the water cleansing you while washing away your negative energy.

Chant these words while the water is pouring over you in the shower. Begin by taking deep breaths, breathing deeply to inhale fresh clear air and blowing outward any stagnant energy when exhaling. Then say aloud:

Mother Earth grounds me,
This deep breath restores me,
The rays of Father Sun nourish me.
This pure water renews me.
I am filled with Pure Light as I journey forward.
(Touch your forehead)
Let my mind open to the truth.
(Touch your lips)
Let my lips speak the truth.
(Touch your heart area)
Let my heart seek the ways of pure love, now and always.
(Touch each palm)
Let my hands be gifted to work in healing ways.
(Touch the sole of each foot)
Let my feet ever walk upon the sacred path.

Exit the shower, wrap yourself in a robe, and find a comfortable place to relax. Light a candle and drink some natural spring water. When you are ready, begin a fifteen-minute meditation, asking your guides to share a message they have for you this night. At the end of fifteen minutes, thank your guides and end the meditation and prepare for a good night's sleep.

While this ritual is dynamic, rejuvenating, and renewing anywhere it is celebrated, it has been said that nowhere on Earth is this magic stronger than in New Orleans, due to its unique location at the mouth of the Mississippi River, as the energy pours forth from the river into the Gulf of Mexico, with New Orleans serving as a crescent bowl gathering and holding the energy. The ceremonies performed in connection with this powerful connection with water are similar to the ones performed in the times of ancient Egypt along the Nile.

To stimulate the fire energy of purification around your auric fields on a daily basis, keep a Himalayan salt lamp in a room that you occupy each day or evening. The combination of fire and salt creates negative ions and powerful purifying energy for both you and your home.

Ten

HOW TO SENSE
SPIRIT GUIDES IN
THE AURIC FIELDS

What lies behind us and what lies before us are
tiny matters compared to what lies within us.
—Ralph Waldo Emerson

There is an old Buddhist proverb that says, "When the student is ready, the teacher will appear." While this can be frustrating to hear at times, there is great truth behind this teaching. Many people also say, "You only find love when you are not looking for it," and the same wisdom applies here. There are thousand of stories from people who looked for love everywhere, but only after they stopped looking for that special someone did love find them. You may even experience this on a minor daily level, when you search high and low for a seemingly lost item, such as a book, but only find it after you have given up all hope of seeing your favorite old paperback ever again.

The same analogy can be applied when looking to connect with your guides. Your spirit guides are by your side for your lifetime, but learning how to communicate with them can be difficult at first. The main reason we have difficulty sensing them is that we try too hard and overthink the process. As we focus with determination, we activate the mental field to the point that it overshadows the other fields. Communicating with your spirit guides comes from accessing the higher planes. In order to do this, you have to free your mind and allow your intuitive energy body to take over.

If we were speaking in Eastern philosophical terms, I would say, "Do not look for a guide; rather, allow the guide to find you." To do this, you must relax and remain observant and open. As you do, you will find that your guides have been with you every day of your life. They have spoken to you through the interactions of your day with each person you encounter, teaching you more about yourself as a human and spiritual being. There is great reverence and depth of understanding in allowing each relationship to guide and inspire you in each moment. Your guides also speak with you through your auric fields, causing you to have a gut reaction to something, or a sudden intuitive feeling to go somewhere (or not go there), or to reach out and connect with a person whom you were not thinking about previously.

While focusing your energy on learning from each and every person you meet and interact with on a daily basis, your mind will open and your consciousness will expand, which allows for the wisdom of the Universe to come pouring into you from the great repository. As you are open to this process, your guides are able to send direct messages to you through these interactions and daily encounters. When you have, as the ancient teachings say, "the eyes with which to see and the ears with which to hear," you will recognize the signs and communications being presented to you along the path.

Your higher self already knows all of the answers you seek. Your guide is there to help you reach within and remove the shroud covering these answers. Believe that the answers you seek are coming to you now, and they will appear. Be sure to keep an open mind and understand that they may not appear in the form you expect. If you look too hard in one direction, you may miss the guidance coming to you from another source.

In this chapter, we are going to explore a variety of exercises that you can use to connect with your spirit guides through your auric field. It is also important to note that the very act of conscious thought will now activate the connection between you and your spirit guides. Once you have the conscious connection with your energy fields, which you have been creating with every exercise in this book, the wall between the layers is being lifted and you are able to sense and connect with your auric fields. As this ability develops, you can now "ask" your spirit guides to appear, and they will find ways to appear to you in the manner they think is most beneficial for you. This mode of appearance will alter and change over time, as you develop and raise your vibrational energy.

Spirit Guides

Spirit guides come in various forms. There is a hierarchy on the spiritual planes, and different guides are assigned to their various occupations. The connection begins with a review of your akashic records, which is a conscious grid in the higher spiritual planes that records each experience we have on the earthly plane during our lifetimes, down to the level of every thought, word, action, and deed. It also makes a record of how we felt emotionally with every action and thought, and how we made others feel emotionally with every thought, word, action, and deed we expressed toward them.

Each lifetime, before we return to the earthly plane, we meet with our spiritual advisors on the Other Side and review our akashic records. Our actions during each lifetime create what is called karma. This

universal law dictates that for every action, there is an equal and opposite reaction, and we return to experience these reactions and to create
new actions and learn further. In order to successfully undertake this
adventure, we are assigned a team of spiritual coaches, often referred to
as "spirit guides."

On average, most people are assigned between three and seven main
spirit guides who watch over them in their lifetime. While these are
your main guides, others are called in at times for specific purposes and
duties and then may never be seen again in the same lifetime. When
we pass on from this lifetime, we meet with our spiritual coaching team
again. At this meeting, we review how we advanced in this lifetime and
what new opportunities this brings for our future. We also consider
and feel the weight of the negative decisions we made and discuss what
we'll need to do in the next lifetime to make restitution and correct
these mistakes.

There are a wide variety of guides around you in each lifetime. As
we discussed, some stay with us for the entire lifetime and others visit
only when needed. Let's look at some of the types of guides.

Inspirational Spirit Guides

The energy of these spirit guides is filled with joy and serenity. Being
in their presence feels dreamy and elusive. They bring hope and remind
you why it feels good to be here with all the wonder and beauty in the
world. By nature and design, these guides float around us only spo-
radically. They are only here to remind us of joy, the power of love, and
what it means to be fully alive and present in the moment. They cannot
stay in our energy fields for too long, because we would become too
attached to their presence. Such an attachment would cause us to want
to withdraw from the rest of the world and spend all of our time communicating with these inspirational spirit guides.

The energy they exude feels like a beautiful dream. Their beautiful energy can be remembered forever but only experienced for a few

moments on the earthly plane. These guides visit you to remind you of the spiritual planes and that, at times, life can be like heaven on Earth. They are natural forces and must do what they do; they cannot be contained as they move quickly around the earthly plane, spreading their light and joy. Once this blissful moment is experienced, they must drift away or you will become enraptured and stay caught in stasis instead of moving forward with your life. Their purpose is to create a magical moment of bliss, to remind people that the energy from the higher planes is always accessible and can exist on Earth.

You can't ask these guides to come to you; they appear in their own time. You can sense them when they enter your auric field and can see them in another's auric field. They sparkle and appear like incandescent orbs of light in the auric field.

Teaching Spirit Guides

Chances are that if you are reading books like this, you have been on a spiritual journey for some time and are connecting with your higher self. Along this path, once your consciousness has been awakened, your guides become excited because the connection is opening further and they can engage and communicate with you more directly. While they are never allowed to tell you what to do (it would interfere with free will and your destiny), they can offer advice and help you to understand what is occurring in your life.

Teaching spirit guides were assigned to you before you returned to the earthly plane for this lifetime. As you and your spiritual team were going over your life path and destiny plan for this lifetime, you met and chose the guides that you felt would be able to best help you on your journey. Teaching guides are meant to be tough on you. They are by your side when you are going through each experience and offer a nudge to move you in the right direction. Their prime directive is to help you release old patterns and karmic imprints that no longer serve you. They work to help you uncover deep-rooted energetic patterns that you are ready to release and transform. When they appear around your energy field, it is like a clap of thunder. You feel awake and energized and ready to pay attention and make a change.

The easiest way to connect with your teaching guides is to first see them in meditation. Begin by visualizing a space that is relaxing and peaceful, perhaps a park or garden setting with trees and flowers. See a bench in this setting and sit down on the bench. Looking out over the scenery, ask that your guide appear to you. When I engage in this activity, my guide sits on the bench next to me and we have a chat about the world and life. He often brings a bag of bread with him and we tear it up into small pieces to feed to the ducks in the nearby pond while discussing my next move.

You will find with every example and exercise given to you in this book, the more you practice, the more easily the connection will form. Each time you work with the auric fields, your intuitional energy is enhanced, the connection to your higher self is increased, and the channels open further to meet with your guides.

Exercise: Connecting with Your Guides

When we are faced with stressful situations, the emotional auric body takes on energy before it filters down into the physical body. When our auric bodies become overwhelmed with a constant flow of negative or stressful energy, it can be more difficult to become a clear channel to receive assistance from our guides, even though they are always with us and ready to assist.

If you communicate regularly with your guides but find that you are unable to connect with them occasionally when you are stressed, there is an easy way to reconnect. This practice works well for people who have already established a connection, but it can also be used if you have never connected with your guides before and want to attempt to connect. The practice is to sleep on it. Follow these steps:

Step One: Early in the day, prepare the bedroom, making it as comfortable and cozy as possible. Remove any clutter from the room and bring in quilts and pillows to snuggle up with. Purchase an aromatherapy lavender spray and lightly spray the pillowcases and sheets. Place a pad and pen on the table next to the bed, so that when you wake in the morning, you can write down all the dreams you can remember before getting out of bed. This is also helpful if you wake up in the middle of night from having a dream, as you can write or draw as much information as you can recall from the dream and ask to remember even more details in the morning.

Step Two: When you are ready to go to sleep, find a comfortable position and relax. Take three deep breaths in, pulling in fresh clear air. While breathing in, you should be able to smell the lavender around you. With each exhale, release any stagnant energy from within you and let go of your thoughts and cares from the day. Next, softly speak aloud a prayer of protection three times while surrounding yourself with white light. Relax and feel your body letting go. You are at peace and all is well in your world. Relax and breathe deeply.

Step Three: Visualize the sacred space you've created from the meditation exercise in chapter seven, such as the garden with a bench where your guide often meets with you. As you visualize your sacred space, ask your guides to visit you in your dreams this evening as you sleep. Ask them to work with you so that you are open to understand what they are about to communicate to you. Then, affirm to yourself that you will remember your dreams in the morning.

Step Four: When you wake, it's important to write down as much detail about each of your dreams as you can remember, no matter how trivial or silly it seems at the time. Later in the day, review what you've written and see what clues are being presented in the dream. If you don't have much practice with dream interpretation, there are many books available on the subject describing symbols and what they can mean in dreams.

Step Five: Keep a journal of your dreams. You may find that as you look over the journal entries a week or month later, you will understand more as you look at the progression of dreams over a period of time. It's important to remember that it can take time to establish the connection and remember your dreams upon waking. Communicating in the dream state takes practice, just like any other skill. If you keep up this work (once a week is a good place to start), you will get better over time and the communication with your guides will begin to flow on an easier level.

Exercise: Seeing Spirit Guides in the Auric Field

Once you have mastered seeing the auric fields and discerning the colors in the aura, the next step is to see the presence of spirit guides in the auric fields. These beings appear in a wide variety of forms and sizes. When looking at someone's aura, here's how to detect beings in the field, including those that wish to be seen and those that don't:

Step One: Surround yourself with white light and expand your auric force field so that you have a strong protective shield around your fields and body. You are about to attempt to communicate with beings from the Other Side. While most of them are overwhelmingly beautiful beings of light, there are also other beings out there; before doing any work of this kind, it is always best to protect yourself and raise your auric shield.

Step Two: Light a candle in the room where you will be conducting the reading. The light of the fire serves to illuminate the fields and purify the energy during the reading.

Step Three: Begin reading the auric field of the person. As you see the colors and movements in the auric fields, watch for any distinguishing patterns, which move quickly around the fields. The most noticeable types are sparkles that resemble tiny stars and orbs of white light. The orbs may also streak across the body, leaving a white trail across one of the auric fields. When you encounter a sparkling presence or white light orb, ask the presence if it is willing to show itself to you in a more complete form. There is no need to ask this out loud—you are communicating telepathically with the being and can ask the question in your mind, directing your energetic thought from your fields.

Step Four: Should the being choose to engage with you, it will usually grow larger in size and take on the appearance of a human or angelic form. They often choose a form that they feel will help you and your client best understand who they are or what type of work they represent as a guide or spiritual being in the person's auric field. At this point, if the person whose auric field you are reading is willing, you can ask questions of their guide and invite the person to ask questions out loud as well. You can function as the interpreter, passing along the information. The person may also wish to ask the guide to engage with them more often and can invite them to visit them in their dreams so they can create a stronger relationship and establish a line of communication.

Step Five: While speaking to the guide or guides, ask if there is any information to be passed along to the person you are reading for, including the health and well-being of their physical, mental, and emotional bodies.

Step Six: During this consultation, ask the guides whether there are any areas where negative energy is residing and if it has attracted any energy feeders, which attach themselves to one of the levels of the auric fields. If the guide indicates that there are, ask the person you are reading for if they would like to work with their guide now in order to clear and cleanse their auric layers and remove negative energy from their fields. If the person agrees, have them say three times out loud:

> *I am surrounded by the pure white light.*
> *Nothing but good can come to me,*
> *nothing but good can come from me.*
> *I give thanks.*

As they are saying this out loud, ask their guide to assist in raising the white light energy field around the body, so that it increases in intensity. When this occurs, it creates a spiritual fire that burns off lower vibrational energy, consuming and eliminating the negative energy in the fields. The heat and high energy instantly repel any lower-level energy feeders who have attached themselves to the field, and they must flee or risk being burned. This is why it is very important to surround yourself in a strong auric shield before you begin this work, and that you only attempt this type of aura reading when you are in a high energy and positive state. Doing this exercise when you yourself are experiencing low energy or are without a shield may cause the removed being to simply attach onto you instead of the person whose aura you are reading.

Step Seven: Take three deep breaths in and out and thank the spirit guides for their assistance. Close your eyes for a moment to end the connection while taking another three deep breaths. Then open your eyes and stand up, releasing any energy around you down into the ground. Invite the person you were reading for to stand and do the same. You both should be feeling very positive and full of energy at this time, as the energy has been restored for the person and the presence of the beings from the higher planes has been magnified through them into the room. Extinguish the candle and the practice is complete. You may wish to eat a bit of dark chocolate or drink a bit of pure water at this time to ground yourself back in the physical realm.

Eleven

EXPERIENCING THE
AURA EVOLUTION

Then indecision brings its own delays
And days are lost lamenting o'er lost days.
Are you in earnest? Seize this very minute;
What you can do, or dream you can, begin it;
Boldness has genius, power, and magic in it.
—Johann Wolfgang von Goethe

Life appears these days to be moving at the speed of sound and gaining momentum each day. New discoveries reveal that electrons may be able to spin faster than the speed of light, thus challenging widely held scientific theories that say such speed is impossible. As we enter a new understanding of global consciousness in our role as creators, we are transcending time and space as we knew it to exist before and entering into a new state of being.

A marker of this future change of the ages is the year 2012, and the discussions, musings, and prophecies of what will occur during this time proliferate. In the ancient wisdom teachings, it is said that the changes of each age unfold over a long period of time, with certain dates marked along the way as displaying significant shifts of energy in connection with the new age.

In this book, we've looked at the past century and how the Industrial Revolution has affected our auric bodies. We've also looked back at how the Dark Ages contributed to our loss of knowledge and connection with our auric bodies, and how we've been actively engaged in restoring this information and ancient wisdom.

Along with the difficult times, the human race has also been in the process of evolving and experiencing great shifts of consciousness and change. One example is the Renaissance Age and another is the 1960s with the "peace and love" movement. The evolution is proceeding onward through today and gaining momentum quickly!

Where We're Heading

Our future has science and spirituality working together to unravel the mysteries of the Universe. Spiritual mystics have shared universal truths since ancient times, and now the general consciousness of humanity is open to receiving this knowledge. This knowledge becomes available to us not only in the mental field, but as we shift from the third dimension into the fourth and fifth dimensions, we will receive and understand information through all of the auric fields on a greater scale. During this new age of enlightenment in which we are living, science is beginning to catch on to what the mystics have been teaching for centuries and is discovering tangible ways to study these teachings through quantum physics.

We've discussed the hermetic axiom "As Above, So Below" and how this works with the auric fields. If we look at our soul and the auric fields, as they fully exist, they extend far beyond the seven planes that we've discussed, which are closest around the body. The "As Above, So Below" analogy can best be used here to liken the auric fields to the shape of an upside-down pyramid. The pyramid's large base is up in the spiritual planes, where souls go when they leave the earthly plane. The tiny capstone (tip) of the pyramid is the section that resides within your body, in the heart. This capstone contains the spark of life, the life force that activates the soul and begins to pour all that is you from the higher planes down into your heart when you are born.

As you can imagine, this is a lot of energy and information to absorb, so the process slows as the pyramid grows narrower until it reaches the tip inside of you. This capstone has a crystalline structure that captures all of the experiences in your life and returns this energy information back up to the higher planes and stores them in the akashic records.

From this capstone, a second pyramid is generated right-side up, which encapsulates the auric fields around our body down to the ground. The two pyramids interconnect at each capstone in the heart and are joined through the energy cords and meridians throughout the body. This ancient teaching has been symbolized in many forms, including the Star of David, the tetrahedron, and the Flower of Life.

Here on the earthly plane, we currently ground through the lower chakras. We tend to think of the spiritual planes as places above us in the sky, where people point when they are speaking of heaven. There are many levels to the higher planes, but they can be reached from various points of your body, including your heart, throat, and third-eye region. The higher planes are closer and more accessible than most people realize. In the higher planes, the confining rules of the earthly plane do not exist, including the limitations of time as well as the concept of being in one space at one time. The higher one moves into the spiritual planes, the greater the ability to be omnipresent. This allows us, basically, to be in several places at once. The first plane where this ability appears is in the astral field.

As we take this big-picture look at the auric fields, we see that the majority of the essence and energy of what makes us who we are resides in the higher planes, and that only a small portion of that energy trickles down into the body. The majority of our essence and soul energy remains in the higher planes with a much greater consciousness and awareness, making up the sum of all of our parts, lifetimes, and experiences.

When we reach out to speak to a loved one who has passed on, we connect with this part of their essence, what we would refer to as their Higher Self. The Higher Self retains memory of all lifetimes, including the energy of who this person was in the lifetime we remember them from. This aspect of the person then appears to us in their energetic form with access to all the memories and experiences from this lifetime.

The Eighth Auric Field and Chakra

Beyond the classical seven chakras, there is an eighth chakra, also referred to as the soul star chakra. The auric energy field connected to this chakra stores the energy of the akashic records and karma. It is the last field to hold energy from your present human life and the essence of you in this lifetime. As we are evolving into the new age of enlightenment, the eighth chakra has become more engaged and active in our auric fields. It is responding to the universal energy, which is speeding up. For every action there is a reaction, and we are currently experiencing the reaction in our body, mind, and spirit. The eighth chakra oversees karma and disperses information from the akashic records, which allows us to experience situations to work off our karma. As the energy has intensified and magnified, we are burning off karmic debt at the highest rate ever experienced. In the past, it could take lifetimes to burn off karma; in this lifetime, it can take just days.

The eighth auric field and chakra also hold the energy that I explain to my students in this teaching:

> *We are all One, One Energy, from One Light.*
> *Let us band together as humans with love for all*
> *of humanity, living each day in harmony as we*
> *explore our spirit.*

The eighth chakra holds the energetic field where we no longer function in the concept of "me, me, me." The focus is on global consciousness and connectedness with all beings. The evolutionary rate at which this chakra and auric field are now vibrating is affecting every person here on Earth. Much of what we see happening around us on very negative global scales are the result of this vibrational energy shaking up all the old patterns in order to destroy them. This destruction is necessary in order to cleanse, purify, and prepare the way for the new energy to come in and assist in the shift from the third dimension. In ancient times, it would be said that the goddess Kali (from the Hindu religion) or the goddess Sekhmet (from the ancient Egyptian teachings) had been unleashed to do her work. The Hindu religion describes it as the end of the age of Kali Yuga, which has been an age where human civilization and society degenerates spiritually. Signs of being in the age of Kali Yuga are wars and injustices to humanity and a complete lack of character, such as was seen in the Dark Ages.

The Evolution of the Auric Fields

Since 1999, I've observed new crystalline structures forming in the aura that I have never seen in the human aura field before. It appears that our spiritual bodies are evolving at a rapid pace that could be referred to as a "quickening," and our energy bodies are being attuned right before our very eyes. Our energy bodies are being reconstructed and are opening up to allow more light and energy to flow through our bodies than ever before.

These structures are creating new energy cords, which form a grid around the auric body. Beginning in 2006, I began to observe these cords connecting, expanding, and vibrating in the auric fields of many people with significantly greater energy. The grid and the cord connection are highly conscious and interactive. They respond to conscious contact both from the individual who is aware of this new field around them and from others who engage in communication with the cords on an intuitive level.

The cords connect in three places inside the body: the solar plexus chakra, the heart chakra, and above the head. The area above the head does not interact directly with the crown chakra; it is connected with the higher planes, where information and light flows directly into the aura, which is the eighth chakra. The completed grid shape has cords of light extending from the chakras into the newly formed grid around the body.

The three main cords expand and connect with smaller cords coming from each of the other chakras and from the internal organs. They connect to the grid and then extend farther outward to connect with cords coming from the higher levels of the energy bodies and beyond. These cords then extend their connections outward. Each cord has to "grow," and when a cord grows long enough to reach the other cords, it "snaps together" tightly, creating a new grid system around the person.

I refer to this new structure as the "higher consciousness grid," and the speed at which it is evolving is fascinating. Each time I view one of these almost fully formed grids on someone I'm reading, I see more neuronlike networks connecting into the grid. The structures are expanding the auric field, from the old form of the oval shape around the body into a more expansive grid system connected by the cords. The cords are able to stretch and grow and have tendrils, which can reach out to create new patterns. It appears to me to be a much stronger system, with the cords forming the grid, and light and energy running through the cords at a much faster rate than the old auric fields.

Intuitively, it feels as if our consciousness is being gathered through these cords and a ship is being created around each of us to transport our consciousness and essence to a different place.

If there was ever a time I wondered about how we would manage to shift from the third dimension into the fourth and fifth, I no longer have any of those concerns, as I see the actual energetic transportation devices being built around people every day in preparation for this evolution.

The consciousness grids—or "ships" as I call them—vary in size and strength. The most fully formed grids I have seen are emerging from people who emit the strongest energy from their heart chakra area. These grids, which are able to fully extend from the heart chakra, form a strong, double-walled oval shape around the body, with a malleable texture and beautiful glow. These structures pulse with energy and a vibrant light. The colors of the aura can be seen through this grid and there are new colors coming from the interior of these cords.

The heart chakra grid is one of several types of grid structures being formed in the auric field. Some people are not quite ready to open their heart chakra to the point of this energetic vibration. In these cases, grid systems are formed using a complex system of connections that run through the three lower chakras. The colors and sizes of these cords vary accordingly. For those who are not quite ready to move from the solar plexus chakra into the heart chakra energetic level, the grid appears to be shaping the new body of each person using the solar plexus chakra as the base point.

This transition is creating an energetic transformation in the person. It is significant and similar to what the ancient Egyptians referred to as the power of the light body to do "magic" in order for humanity to evolve into light beings.

How the Cords Operate

In the solar plexus chakra, there is a large cord extending outward from the physical body; this cord is not connected to the new grid system. Instead, it hangs down from the solar plexus (giving the appearance of a belt tied around your waist with the excess of the belt hanging downward).

This cord appears to function as an exit valve, allowing emotional energy to be released and removed from the body. This was the first new cord I noticed on people, as it was much larger than other energy cords I had seen previously around the body. It appears to be important that this exit valve be in place first, as it releases the lower vibrational energy connected with fear, anger, and other emotions and impulses from the first, second, and third chakras and auric fields. This process has speeded up, and many people are experiencing physical symptoms in connection with these three chakras as their energy bodies work to remove the emotional pain connected with and stored in these chakras.

For the people who are not yet comfortable opening their heart chakra fully at this time, a grid is still being constructed in a slower level around their auric fields. In order to help this process, smaller cords, which look like tendrils rather than full cords, are emerging from their solar plexus area. These cords help the person to release their fear and remove the pain they have experienced over lifetimes. These small cords connect and work in conjunction with the larger solar plexus exit valve. They also connect into the fourth level of the auric layer and allow the connection to the akashic records to be accessed more easily by the person. This is why karmic actions and reactions that once took lifetimes to experience now happen in weeks and, in some cases, days. Many people report the awareness that time is speeding up, and it certainly appears that this is the case with the aura and energy bodies, as they are more active than I have ever seen before.

This active growth and evolutionary period of our light bodies affects each person differently. Some people are reporting physical sensations in their body that they cannot explain, including periods of dizziness, fatigue, anxiety, panic attacks, feelings of their heart racing, and other symptoms that their doctors are unable to diagnose the cause of. Others have medical disorders that pop up and then go away almost as quickly.

As with any evolution and change, there are side effects experienced during a period of rapid growth.

Once this cord from the solar plexus is formed and fully functioning as an exit valve, the forming of the consciousness grid begins. A new cord emerges from the heart chakra. The heart cord looks similar to a tendril from a plant. It is activated when the heart stirs and awakens in a moment of pure joy or love. It is as simple and exquisite as this—one moment of pure joy or love can activate this cord.

As this cord emerges from the heart chakra, it continues to grow, being fed from the light and energy emitted by the person, along with the light around the person stored in their auric body. This first sprout of the cord is soft and it curls as it expands from the heart chakra. As it grows, it straightens out into a firm cord, similar to the stalk of a plant.

Once the cord reaches a level of mature growth, it attaches to the first layer of the aura body. Now the heart chakra is connected directly into the aura through this cord. In many ways, it reminds me of the experience that I see with the cords that connect from the fourth layer when a mother and child connect cords. This cord from the heart comes from Divine Feminine energy and is creating a womb around the body, so that each of her children may be reborn.

As the heart cord expands and thickens, the person operates more from their higher auric fields and chakras and less energy is released from the lower chakras through the solar plexus cord. As the person expresses more of their energy from the higher fields, the solar plexus cord begins to shrink in thickness and length. I have not seen a person who has completely eliminated this cord from their solar plexus, but I have seen the cord shrinking substantially on some people. My belief is that, like an umbilical cord, it will soon shrink to the size where it connects through the belly button and eventually drops off, as does the umbilical cord on a baby.

The steady progress of the consciousness grids continues to expand with even greater momentum and speed. Since 2006, I've observed that the new structures surrounding the auric field and energy bodies appear different in people according to their age and state of well-being. What I have seen forming in all stages of life is overwhelmingly positive and awe-inspiring and appears to constitute a virtual evolution of our light bodies.

The higher consciousness grid is beginning to extend cords and tendrils.

CReleasing the CDark in Order to CEmbrace the Coming Light

In early 2001, I began sharing with my students my impression that there would be a difficult period of time coming. The energy would feel thick, heavy, and dark and finding the energy to conduct light work and spiritual training would feel more challenging. I shared that the most difficult time would be during 2007 through 2014, as this time would test people down to their core beliefs, morals, and values, including their sense of self and their personal strength to endure what they see going on around them in the world. Many people understand and are experiencing this difficulty right now, as it simply feels harder to do things they previously did with ease on a daily basis.

Part of the vibrational energy that I speak of is coming from the ethers—the etheric realms and beyond—and is causing an effect at this time that is felt by all things on Earth and resonates in our auric bodies and in nature. We are in a period of rapid evolution. In order to evolve, we first must cleanse and purify our surroundings and ourselves energetically. In a very rudimentary and basic example, I describe the concept of a junk closet in the home. In this closet are lots of things that we need and use often, yet no one wants to take the time to clean out the closet, go through what we no longer need, discard it, and reorganize the items. We are so caught up in our daily activities that we avoid taking the time to clean out the closet. Our minds are so busy that we are unable to see that cleaning it out would actually give us more time in our daily life, since we wouldn't waste time pulling out half of the junk in the closet to find the one thing we are looking for on a given day. Instead, we allow the clutter to grow in the closet, convincing ourselves that we don't have the time to deal with the problem. One day, the clutter becomes so great that we can no longer shove anything else inside and when we open the door, the enormity of the mass of things falls upon us.

In the same way, our auric fields are storage containers, our "clos-
ets," and they can hold the great amount of energy we place inside of
them. For many lifetimes now, we have been able to continue to place
more emotional and mental baggage as well as old karmic debt into
these fields and pull them out as we choose. We have chosen to keep
stuffing things into the fields, deciding we'll deal with them on another
day, and we just pull out what we need day after day. With the new age
coming from the Divine Feminine, the Great Mother is saying that we
cannot continue as we have been. In a grand cosmic way, we cannot
move forward and go outside of our lower auric fields to play until we
have cleaned our closet (our auric fields).

We are being provided with tools in our aura to help us accomplish
this work, and the extended cord from the solar plexus is helping us
to release this energy. The effects of this evolution are being felt by all
beings on Earth. Crystals are natural receivers, and they are document-
ing these changes and absorbing the effects. I believe that what is being
seen in the crystals at this time is similar to what Masaru Emoto, author
of *The Hidden Messages in Water,* found in his research. His research
indicated that the structure of water crystals was affected through positive and negative energy directed toward the water by human words,
thoughts, and intentions. The theory suggests that water as a conductor
of energy (which covers most of our planet as well as making up a large
percentage of our body) reacts to human energy, and thus the tumult
that we see with water is in part a reaction to the global consciousness.
With this thought in mind, crystals may very well be indicating the
same receptivity to the energy being felt and expressed so strongly during this time.

My guides tell me that it is the evolutionary changes that we as
humans are experiencing that are causing these rippling effects, along
with the turbulent energy in the etheric realms that is now presenting
itself on the earthly plane.

If you choose to work with crystals during this time, be aware of the energy they are receiving and choose the best quality crystal you can find. Quartz crystals amplify the energy that a person puts into them. They can be charged with intention and energy and will magnify this intention. This includes healing, protection, peace, balance, and really whatever you wish to put into the crystal. I'm careful in my work with them, since they magnify energy. I have quartz crystal bowls that sing and I feel it is important to only play them when there is a sense of reverence and intent because they are so energetically malleable.

What's Coming in the New Decade

Happy New You! This new decade heralds a new cycle of energy, further releasing the past and opening the door to unlimited possibilities. It brings a major shift to the masses in regard to conscious thinking and opens the door to further self-realization and heightened psychic awareness and abilities.

Time has been moving at an unparalleled rate, which thus far in the twenty-first century has brought us the gift of seeing our hopes, dreams, thoughts, and wishes manifest at a surprising and sometimes alarming rate. Truly this current decade has focused on manifesting the belief that **if we can think it, we can achieve it.**

As we've dared to dream and open our mind, the shift of ages from Pisces to Aquarius is gifting us with a never-before-seen outpouring of information. No longer are we reliant upon a particular university, library, or reference text to provide information. From the spiritual planes above, Aquarius has tipped the waters of illumination and knowledge from the gods back down to Earth for us to receive. Thanks to the air sign of Aquarius, we have seen this information fly quickly through the Internet, connecting humanity on a global scale and providing information on any topic we can conceive of, at any time, with multiple resources to consider and cross-reference. With this gift of knowledge in the new millennium, we've shared our life stories, bonded in social networks, blogged our thoughts, shopped and supported local and global businesses whose storefronts we may never see in person, learned about cultures throughout the world, and tweeted our thoughts to thousands just as quickly as we think them.

The millennium and this decade is deemed the Age of Information and truly it has been—so much so that many people now complain of information overload with so much available.

What will the next decade bring? We are being set free in body, mind, and spirit to let go of our past and explore. We are able to release all karmic ties and bindings and step into a higher field of consciousness to operate from our higher energy bodies, rather than being tied to the emotional and lower mental aspects of our nature. The bridge between the lower level auric fields and the higher fields is open, and we can operate from our astral field with greater ease and expand our psychic abilities.

Those who fail to see the opportunity being offered at this time will regret in the future what they did not dare to try. As Mark Twain said, "Twenty years from now you will be more disappointed by the things that you didn't do than by the ones you did do. So throw off the bowlines. Sail away from the safe harbor. Catch the trade winds in your sails. Explore. Dream. Discover."

In our evolution into Higher Level Conscious Spiritual Beings, we've spent this decade becoming Conscious Creators, playing with the new toys we've received on a basic, rudimentary level.

Beginning in 2020, the journey evolves as we move from knowledge into wisdom. What is the big difference between knowledge and wisdom, you ask? Knowledge is the awareness of the information. Wisdom is gained from taking the knowledge, putting it into action, observing how the action causes various reactions, and then gaining discernment of how it best can be used. A person may be knowledgeable without being wise. Humanity must now begin to develop discernment from our vast stores of information in order to become wise.

As I have shared earlier, we are moving into a new Age of Enlightenment in this new decade. The Aquarian information from the gods can no longer be contained, the Divine Feminine is being released in all her glory, and we will once again see a Renaissance period, where great art, architecture, philosophy, literature, and science will develop and flourish. During this decade, the greatest minds will stir to share, to illuminate, and to build and create works and ideas that will be admired around the world.

You are one of these Creators. If you have been waiting for a sign, if you have wondered "When is my time?"—this is it. We have arrived. The year 2020 is your destiny date, your time to shine. Fly boldly now in the direction of your dreams and use all the resources at your disposal— your aura and your ability to read the aura of others, first and foremost. In this decade, we will connect mind, body, and spirit into the higher auric fields and spiritual realms as the ancients did, connecting with our muses, using our intuition and dreams to guide us, and working in tandem on the spiritual and earthly planes.

It's here, we're here, and this coming decade will be one of history-making on every level.

Afterword

WE ARE ALL ONE

Matter is Energy, Energy is Light. We are all
light beings.

—Albert Einstein

From the civilizations of Lemuria and Atlantis to ancient Egypt, India, and Greece, mystery schools have shared their wisdom and light on Earth. These schools are still in existence, working in various forms of service to humanity, both in the seen and unseen realms. As humanity evolves, the teachings continue to offer their wisdom for those who are ready to enter the temple and become a student of the esoteric teachings.

As a wisdom teacher, I share the esoteric teachings and ancient mysteries at my mystery school, the Temple of Stella Maris. These lessons are as timely today as they were thousands of years ago. Students who wish to explore their inner selves enter the temple, begin the journey to discover who they are, and study topics including the alchemical transformations of the heart, body, and mind; the magical Universe in which we reside; the long-forgotten destiny of our souls; our various bodies of energy; and wisdom lessons from the mystery temples of ancient Egypt, Greece, and other powerful and sacred temples from around the world.

Over the years, I've taught workshops and lectured around the United States about these sacred mysteries. In this age of information and communication, enlightened souls are exploring new concepts and redefining their beliefs as they evolve, including a return to the ancient practices of introspection and observation and looking within for the answers.

Each lesson I present opens the communication between this world and the other realms, activating the energy of the pyramids and the sacred temples, and drawing forth the wisdom of the ancient ones. What I do as a teacher is to help people remember what they already know on a soul level. Each person retains this information deep within their soul, where they hold the keys to universal wisdom.

Beyond sharing the esoteric mystery teachings, I embrace a vision of "Many Paths, One Destination," meaning that each person walks their individual path but all seek to know more about themselves, their world, and what is beyond this world. This is the vision of my talk show, *The Explore Your Spirit with Kala Show* (ExploreYourSpirit.com), where I interview world-renowned authors, artists, teachers, healers, and researchers delving into metaphysical, supernatural, and paranormal topics as well as new discoveries between science and spirituality. There are hundreds of shows available in the archives and I invite you to enjoy them all if you are so led.

In this new century, life is changing quickly for all of us. It's easy to get caught up in the trials and tribulations of daily life. The intention and energy behind this book is to remind you that **You Are a Divine Light on this Earth.** It is also to offer hope, because what I see for the future of humanity is beyond words in its scope of beauty, form, and function. We truly are light beings, and in the future we will become greater than we remembered ourselves to be.

As you connect with the evolution of your auric body, know that there is a divine destiny and purpose in all that you do. The future is now and it's time to...

Connect and Strengthen Your Light,
Speak with Purpose,
Live Your Highest and Best Thoughts and Dreams,
Love with Abandon,
and
Let Your Light Shine for the World To See.
Hear the Song of Your Heart
and
Feel the Presence of Your Light.
Then, Open Your Heart,
Lift Up Your Head,
and
Sing from your Soul.

We are all One—One Energy from One Light. Let us band together as humans, with love for all of humanity, living each day in harmony as we explore our spirit.

Bibliography

Allen, James. *As a Man Thinketh*. New York: Tarcher, 2007.

Ambrose, Kala. *9 Life Altering Lessons: Secrets of the Mystery Schools Unveiled*. Los Angeles: Reality Press, 2007.

Andrews, Ted. *How to See and Read the Aura*. Woodbury, MN: Llewellyn Worldwide, 2008.

Bailey, Alice. *Esoteric Healing: A Treatise on the Seven Rays*. London: Lucis Publishing, 1972.

Besant, Annie, and C. W. Leadbeater. *Thought-Forms*. New York: Quest Books, 1999.

Birren, Faber. *The Symbolism of Color*. New York: Citadel Press, 1989.

Blavatsky, H. P. *The Secret Doctrine*. New York: Tarcher, 2009.

Brennan, Barbara. *Hands of Light: A Guide to Healing through the Human Energy Field.* New York: Bantam, 1988.

Butler, W. E. *How to Read the Aura.* New York: Weiser, 1971.

Campbell, Joseph. *The Power of Myth.* New York: Anchor Publishing, 1991.

Cayce, Edgar. *Auras.* Virginia Beach, VA: A.R.E. Press, 1945.

De Long, Douglas. *Ancient Teachings for Beginners.* Woodbury, MN: Llewellyn Worldwide, 2007.

Emoto, Masaru. *Hidden Messages in Water.* New York: Atria Books, 2005.

Hall, Manly P. *Melchizedek and the Mystery of Fire.* London: Philosophical Research Society, 1996.

Jones, Alex. *Seven Mansions of Color.* Marina Del Ray, CA: DeVorss and Co., 1982.

Jung, Carl. *Psychology and Alchemy.* New York: Pantheon Books, 1953.

Krippner, Stanley, and Daniel Rubin, eds. *The Kirlian Aura: Photographing the Galaxies of Life.* New York: Anchor Books, 1974.

Kuthumi, Djwal Kul. *The Human Aura.* Livingston, MT: Summit University Press, 1986.

Leadbeater, C. W. *Man: Visible and Invisible.* London: Theosophical Publishing, 1981.

Lilly, Sue, and Simon Lilly. *Healing with Crystals and Chakra Energy.* New York: Barnes and Noble, 2006.

Lipton, Bruce. *The Biology of Belief.* Carlsbad, CA: Hay House, 2008.

Martin, Barbara. *The Healing Power of Your Aura.* Sunland, CA: Spiritual Arts Institute, 2007.

Meyer, Marvin, ed. *The Nag Hammadi Scriptures: The Revised and Updated Translation of Sacred Gnostic Texts Complete in One Volume.* New York: HarperOne, 2009.

Moody, Raymond. *Life after Life.* New York: HarperOne, 2001.

Pauli, Wolfgang, and C. G. Jung. C. A. Meier, ed. *Atom and Archetype: The Pauli/Jung Letters, 1932–1958.* Princeton, NJ: Princeton University Press, 2001.

Powell, A. E. *The Astral Body and Other Astral Phenomena.* New York: Quest Books, 1927.

———. *The Etheric Double.* New York: Quest Books, 1969.

Radin, Dean. *Entangled Minds: Extrasensory Experiences in a Quantum Reality.* New York: Paraview Pocket Books, 2006.

Read, Donna. *The Burning Times.* DVD. Montreal: National Film Board of Canada, 1990.

Shealy, C. Norman. *Life Beyond 100.* Los Angeles: Tarcher, 2006.

Smith, Mark. *Auras: See Them in Only 60 Seconds.* Woodbury, MN: Llewellyn Worldwide, 2008.

Webster, Richard. *Aura Readings for Beginners.* Woodbury, MN: Llewellyn Worldwide, 2007.

Zukav, Gary. *The Dancing Wu Li Masters.* New York: William Morrow, 1979.

———. *The Seat of the Soul.* New York: Free Press, 1990.

Index

GET MORE AT LLEWELLYN.COM

Visit us online to browse hundreds of our books and decks, plus sign up to receive our e-newsletters and exclusive online offers.

- Free tarot readings • Spell-a-Day • Moon phases
- Recipes, spells, and tips • Blogs • Encyclopedia
- Author interviews, articles, and upcoming events

GET SOCIAL WITH LLEWELLYN

Find us on
Facebook
www.Facebook.com/LlewellynBooks

Follow us on
twitter™
www.Twitter.com/Llewellynbooks

GET BOOKS AT LLEWELLYN

LLEWELLYN ORDERING INFORMATION

Order online: Visit our website at www.llewellyn.com to select your books and place an order on our secure server.

Order by phone:
- Call toll free within the U.S. at 1-877-NEW-WRLD (1-877-639-9753)
- Call toll free within Canada at 1-866-NEW-WRLD (1-866-639-9753)
- We accept VISA, MasterCard, and American Express

Order by mail:
Send the full price of your order (MN residents add 6.875% sales tax) in U.S. funds, plus postage and handling to: Llewellyn Worldwide, 2143 Wooddale Drive Woodbury, MN 55125-2989

POSTAGE AND HANDLING:

STANDARD: (U.S. & Canada)
(Please allow 2 business days)
$25.00 and under, add $4.00.
$25.01 and over, FREE SHIPPING.

INTERNATIONAL ORDERS (airmail only):
$16.00 for one book, plus $3.00 for each additional book.

Visit us online for more shipping options.
Prices subject to change.

FREE CATALOG!

To order, call
1-877-NEW-WRLD
ext. 8236
or visit our
website

YOUR
psychic
CHILD

How to Raise
Intuitive
&
Spiritually
Gifted
Kids
of All Ages

"Hands-down, this book is a responsible and positive approach to what can often be a scary subject for
parents and children alike." *Your Psychic Child* might also be called a manual for reaching the Divine."
Meg Blackburn Losey, PhD, author of the internationally best-selling *The Children of Now*

SARA WISEMAN

Your Psychic Child
How to Raise Intuitive & Spiritually Gifted Kids of All Ages
SARA WISEMAN

Want to take an active role in your child's psychic and spiritual development? This indispensable guide helps you to understand and nurture your uniquely gifted children.

Learn about the psychic awakening process and the talents that emerge with each age, from toddler to teen. Discover how to gently encourage your children to explore and develop their strengths in clairvoyance, energy healing, or mediumship. Teach them how to connect with the Divine. Anchored in down-to-earth parental wisdom and alive with personal anecdotes, *Your Psychic Child* is an essential resource for parents who recognize their child's psychic and spiritual potential.

978-0-7387-2061-6, 312 pp., 6 x 9 $17.95

To order, call 1-877-NEW-WRLD
Prices subject to change without notice
Order at Llewellyn.com 24 hours a day, 7 days a week!

Aura
Reading

For Beginners

Develop Your Psychic Awareness for Health & Success

RICHARD WEBSTER

Aura Reading for Beginners
Develop Your Psychic Awareness for Health & Success
Richard Webster

When you lose your temper, don't be surprised if a dirty red haze suddenly appears around you. If you do something magnanimous, your aura will expand. Now you can learn to see the energy that emanates off yourself and other people through the proven methods taught by Richard Webster in his psychic training classes.

Learn to feel the aura, see the colors in it, and interpret what those colors mean. Explore the chakra system, and how to restore balance to chakras that are over- or under-stimulated. Then you can begin to imprint your desires into your aura to attract what you want in your life.

978-1-5671-8798-4, 208 pp., 5³⁄₁₆ x 8   **$12.95**

Discover your Psychic Type

Developing and Using Your Natural Intuition

SHERRIE DILLARD

Discover Your Psychic Type
Developing and Using Your Natural Intuition
SHERRIE DILLARD

Intuition and spiritual growth are indelibly linked, according to professional psychic and therapist Sherrie Dillard. Offering a personalized approach to psychic development, this breakthrough guide introduces four different psychic types and explains how to develop the unique spiritual capabilities of each.

Are you a physical, mental, emotional, or spiritual intuitive? Take Dillard's insightful quiz to find out. Discover more about each type's intuitive nature, personality, potential physical weaknesses, and more. There are guided meditations for each kind of intuitive, as well as exercises to hone your psychic skills. Remarkable stories from the author's professional life illustrate the incredible power of intuition and its connection to the spirit world, inner wisdom, and your higher self.

From psychic protection to spirit guides to mystical states, Dillard offers guidance as you evolve toward the final destination of every psychic type: union with the Divine.

978-0-7387-1278-9, 288 pp., 5³⁄₁₆ x 8   **$14.95**